INTENTIONAL TECH

TEACHING AND LEARNING IN HIGHER EDUCATION
James M. Lang, Series Editor

Other titles in the series:

Intentional Tech

Principles to Guide the Use of Educational Technology in College Teaching

DEREK BRUFF

WEST VIRGINIA UNIVERSITY PRESS

MORGANTOWN 2019

ISBN
Cloth 978-1-949199-15-4
Paper 978-1-949199-16-1
Ebook 978-1-949199-17-8

Library of Congress Cataloging-in-Publication Data is available from
the Library of Congress

Book and cover design by Than Saffel / WVU Press

Contents

Acknowledgments

——————

ONE REASON I love my job is that I get to meet faculty and graduate student instructors from all over academia who teach in such creative and effective ways. I want to thank the following instructors, all thoughtful and intentional teachers, for letting me share their stories in this book: Carwil Bjork-James, Cynthia Brame, Edward Cheng, Elizabeth Cullingford, Robin DeRosa, Larisa DeSantis, Bridget Draxler, Richard Flagan, Timothy Foster, Humberto Garcia, Amanda Golden, Gilbert Gonzales, Erika Grundstrom, Enoch Hale, Ashley Hasty, Alisha Karabinus, Kylie Korsnack, Zoe LeBlanc, Cornelia Lang, Janice Law, Bryan Lowe, Elizabeth Meadows, Ole Molvig, Peter Newbury, Jonathan Rattner, Kimberly Rogers, Margaret Rubega, Tracy Ruscetti, Mark Sample, Mark Schoenfield, Kris Shaffer, Elizabeth Self, Erin Sells, Haerin Shin, Sarah Stiles, Tia Smith, Jeff South, Kathryn Tomasek, Holly Tucker, and Chris Willmott. You inspire me, and I know that your stories will inspire others.

Several of those interviews came about as a result of *Leading Lines*, a podcast on the future of educational technology that I produce with a number of Vanderbilt colleagues. Thanks to those colleagues for always challenging me to think more broadly about educational technology and its role in higher education: Clifford Anderson, Stacey Johnson, Melissa Mallon, Rhett McDaniel, Ole Molvig, Gayathri Narasimham, and John Sloop. Thanks also to my colleagues at the Center for Teaching who teach me so much about teaching, learning, and educational development and have been very patient with me as I vanished from the office for long periods of time to write this book. They are: Joe Bandy, Cynthia Brame, Erica Brandon, Brandon Crawford, Heather Fedesco, Stacey M. Johnson, Rhett McDaniel, Grant Neal, Juliet Traub, and Tracy Tveit. Thanks also to recent Center for Teaching alumni Ashley Burton, Vivian Finch, Nancy Chick, Rebecca Panter, Melissa Penix, and Lee Scarborough, as well as graduate teaching fellows too numerous to name. Thanks to my boss, Cynthia Cyrus, for telling me I should write a book and then making sure I had time to do so. And thanks to the Frothy Monkey coffee shop in Franklin, Tennessee, where I wrote the best parts of this book, and to the "Run Wild" Spotify playlist, my writing soundtrack.

Finally, a very personal thanks to my wife, Emily, for encouraging me, believing in me, and loving me.

Introduction

WHAT TECHNOLOGIES have you used or seen used in teaching contexts? As the director of a teaching center at a research university, I frequently lead workshops on teaching for faculty on my campus and elsewhere. Often, those workshops are focused on teaching with technology, a particular interest of mine. I'll usually open such a workshop with that question about teaching technologies the participants have used or seen, and ask them to respond via a polling system of some kind, using their phones or laptops to submit lists of technologies. The polling system I use assembles the participants' responses in a word cloud, where the more popular a response is, the larger the font size.

Course management systems, like Blackboard and Canvas, are usually in big letters, as are platforms not expressly designed for education, like YouTube, Google, and PowerPoint. Since I wrote a book on polling systems, *Teaching with Classroom Response Systems*, there are usually a number of responses from that category of technology.[1] Other common responses depend on the crowd—scientists tend to mention online homework systems, digital humanists tend to mention Twitter.

Rarely, however, is my favorite educational technology mentioned: wheels on chairs. And by that, I mean classroom furniture, including tables and chairs, that I can easily move around before and during class. When I walk into my classroom, I typically have planned a series of activities for my students focused on my learning objectives for the day. Sometimes that involves whole-class discussion, other times small group work or pair work or a class debate or a jigsaw activity.

Moveable furniture helps me create the kind of classroom environment that supports the learning activities I have planned.

And that's how educational technology should work. Our teaching and learning goals should drive our technology use, not the other way around. As instructors, if we think of ourselves as designers of learning experiences for our students, then we can start to identify technologies and related teaching practices that help to create or enhance those experiences. That is, we should be intentional in how we use technology, looking for ways the technology can support student learning.

Most instructors are comfortable using familiar technologies, like classroom furniture (with or without wheels) and chalkboards and handouts, in intentional ways. When new technologies become available, however, it's not always obvious how to use those technologies in the service of learning. Digital and online technologies in particular compose a landscape that college and university faculty are still surveying, working to determine what's possible and what's useful. As I've talked with faculty across the disciplines about the ways they match technology to pedagogy, a few principles have emerged. In this book, I explore seven teaching principles that can inform and inspire our use of educational technology, digital or otherwise.

What are those principles? Here's a brief preview of the chapters to come:

1. **Times for Telling**—Giving students a hard problem or challenging experience can help them get ready for learning.
2. **Practice and Feedback**—To learn new skills, students need practice applying those skills and to receive feedback on that practice.
3. **Thin Slices of Learning**—The more we understand what and how our students are learning, the more responsive we can be to their learning needs.
4. **Knowledge Organizations**—Providing students with visual ways to organize their knowledge can help them remember and use that knowledge.

5. **Multimodal Assignments**—When students work with new material using different kinds of media, they are better able to learn that material.
6. **Learning Communities**—Structured ways for students to learn from and with each other can enhance the learning experience for all students.
7. **Authentic Audiences**—Connecting students to authentic audiences for their work can motivate students toward deeper learning.

Each chapter focuses on a different principle, and each principle is illustrated with multiple examples of teaching practice, drawn from a variety of disciplines and institutional settings. In my educational development work over the years, I've consulted with hundreds of college and university instructors, and I've interviewed dozens more for this book, for my previous book, and for the educational technology podcast I host, *Leading Lines*.[2] Through these interactions, I've collected stories of intentional, creative, and effective use of technology by faculty and other instructors, and I'm excited to share some of my favorite stories in this book. From my work with faculty, I know that hearing the stories of colleagues can often be the best way to get ideas for one's own teaching. Faculty also like to know that teaching recommendations are based on research, which is why you'll find citations in each chapter pointing to supporting educational research, as well as further reading about concepts and examples.

My goal is to inspire you to be more intentional in how you use technology, whether you've been asked to use a particular technology by an administrator or you've found some shiny new tool you want to try in your classroom or you just want to be more effective at promoting learning and are open to using technology to do so. As a mathematician, I'm drawn to the idea of principles for teaching and learning. Once I've accepted these principles as givens, I can experiment with ways to implement them in my teaching through the activities and assignments I plan for my students. My hope is that you will find these principles relevant and useful, and that the examples in this book will help you see ways you can put them into practice in your teaching. The seven teaching principles explored here are true whether or not we use technology, but they are particularly useful in helping us become more intentional in how we use technologies, old and new, to foster student learning.

CHAPTER 1

Times for Telling

SEVERAL YEARS AGO, my oldest daughter's preschool held a Science Day. Parents were invited to come to school that day and do sciencey things. I volunteered, and I brought along a roll of Mentos breath mints and a two-liter Diet Coke. As the class of five-year-olds stood a safe distance in front of me, I opened the two-liter, poured the sleeve of breath mints in, and jumped back. Half a second later, the soda exploded in an eight-foot-tall geyser. Yes, I was the cool dad who showed the kids what happens when you put Mentos in Diet Coke. As it turned out, the five-year-olds hadn't seen all the viral videos yet.

Then the five-year-olds did what five-year-olds do. They asked, "Why?"

Now, I could have prefaced my demonstration with a ten-minute lecture (with PowerPoint, naturally) on the carbon dioxide dissolved in the soda, the activation energy necessary for that carbon dioxide to transition to gaseous form, the way the breath mint's surface roughness and ready dissolution decrease that activation energy, and the directional foaming of the water caused by all that carbon dioxide gas and the shape of the bottle. Any of the preschoolers still awake at that point would likely have enjoyed the subsequent Diet Coke geyser, but I'm not sure that any of them would have understood or cared about my lengthy explanation. Instead, I led with the demonstration, and when the kids asked "Why?" I offered a simple explanation about gas bubbles in the soda and how the breath mints cause them to come together all at once. That was all the explanation needed that day, and I still got to be the cool dad with the exploding Coke.

But I was struck by how much the order of my actions mattered.

By starting with the demonstration, I had created what Daniel Schwartz and John Bransford call a "time for telling."[1] The preschoolers were ready for an explanation, and they were ready in two ways. Cognitively, they had seen the soda geyser and were thus ready to understand an explanation, at least more ready than they would have been without seeing the geyser. Affectively, they were motivated to hear the explanation. Having seen the geyser, they wanted to know how it worked.

This notion of creating times for telling is one of the most useful teaching principles I share in my consultations with faculty and other instructors. As experts, most of us have an intuition that we should explain first, then have students do something with that explanation. In a literature course, an instructor will lecture on the history and context of a text before having students read that text. In a mathematics course, the professor will present a theorem, then prove the theorem, then show how the theorem applies in a few examples. In an engineering program, students will take a series of courses on engineering principles but wait until senior year to engage in actual design projects. But in many cases, reversing this intuitive order leads to deeper learning.

PRINCIPLE 1. *Giving students a hard problem or challenging experience can help them get ready for learning.*

A few years ago, a group of education researchers at Stanford University led by Bertrand Schneider developed a tabletop simulation of the vision system within the human brain called BrainExplorer.[2] The system featured polymer reproductions of parts of the brain and eyes, along with cameras and infrared lights. This "tangible user interface," as the researchers called it, allowed users to explore the simulated neural network, trying different configurations to discover how light enters the eye and travels to the brain for processing. The researchers took a group of twenty-eight undergraduate and graduate students, none of whom had studied neuroscience, through a sequence of learning activities using BrainExplorer. Half of the students spent time playing with the tabletop simulation, while the other half read textbook-style introductions to the neuroscience of vision. Then the groups switched activities, and were tested on their understanding of the topic. The result? The students who started with BrainExplorer performed 25 percent better than the students who started with text-based explanations. The researchers ran the study again, replacing the text explanations with video explanations, and they got the same results.

Order matters. And, at least in some situations, explanations should follow, not precede, hands-on experience.

Why do students learn better when times for telling are created? For one possible reason, travel with me from Nashville, Tennessee, to the streets of central London. If we stand at a crosswalk on some of those streets and look down at our feet, we will see signs that read "Look Right." These signs likely saved my life more than once during trips to London. As an American, I'm used to road configurations where people drive on the right. That means that when I approach a crosswalk as a pedestrian, my brain expects oncoming traffic to come from the left. The "Look Right" signs in London are helpful reminders that people drive on the other side of the road in London and that I need to look right to check for oncoming cars.

I have in my head, as do you, a mental model of traffic flow. My mental model has been shaped by my experiences living in the United States, where people drive on the right. It's a fine mental model, and it serves me well where I live. But it's the wrong mental model for traffic in London and other places where people drive on the left. When I'm standing at a crosswalk in London that lacks those helpful reminder signs, I can close my eyes, visualize driving on the left, and correct my mental model for the current situation. But changing mental models is hard work. That's why I'm so thankful for those little signs.

In the same way, our students enter our classrooms with all kinds of mental models about how the world works. Some of those mental models are robust and accurate and helpful. Others are incomplete or inaccurate or useful in only certain situations. None of our students enter as blank slates, ready for us to pour information into their heads. Our job as instructors is to help our students develop better mental models, models that are more accurate, more useful, and more flexible to solve the problems our students encounter in the world. But changing mental models is hard work, and we humans aren't inclined to do it. Typically, we don't change our mental models unless directly confronted by some deficiency. When we face a problem our mental models can't help us solve, we're far more open to updating those models and willing to put in the effort to do so.

Lots of people, when confronted by challenges to their mental models, decide not to change. This is why Facebook debates over politics or Twitter arguments over climate change tend to go nowhere. But if we can create for our students experiences where they recognize that their mental models need improving, we can generate times for telling in which students are ready—cognitively and affectively—to change and learn. And when used intentionally, technology can help make that happen.

Bill the Jazz-Playing Accountant

I occasionally teach a statistics course, and in that course I include a unit on probability. Here's a probability question I like to ask my students.

Bill is thirty-four years old. He is intelligent but unimaginative, compulsive, and generally lifeless. In school, he was strong in mathematics but weak in social studies and English. Rank the following statements in order of decreasing likelihood.

A.   Bill is a physician who plays poker for a hobby.
B.   Bill is an architect.
C.   Bill is an accountant.
D.   Bill plays jazz for a hobby.

E. Bill surfs for a hobby.
F. Bill is a reporter.
G. Bill is an accountant who plays jazz for a hobby.
H. Bill climbs mountains for a hobby.

Take a minute and answer the question. List out the statements (A, B, C, and so on) in order, from most likely to be true about Bill to least likely to be true about Bill. I ask my students to do the same, giving them a couple of minutes to work individually on this task.

Then I ask my students to get out their phones. I have a question for them about Bill, and I want them to answer the question using a classroom response system. Classroom response systems are technologies that enable instructors to rapidly collect and analyze student responses to multiple-choice and sometimes free-response questions. In the early years of the twenty-first century, these systems used dedicated handheld devices, often called "clickers," assigned to each student. These days, clicker systems are still available, but many instructors use a bring-your-own-device (BYOD) system that makes use of students' mobile devices—phones and laptops and tablets. Most BYOD systems support text-message responses, so students don't need expensive smart phones, and some systems are free for up to forty students per class, which means such systems are often feasible even in low-resource environments. I use a BYOD system in my stats course, thus my request for students to get out their phones.

Here's the multiple-choice question I give my students, asking them to report out the relationship among three of the statements in their personal ordering:

Which of the following is true for your ranking? Here, > means "is more likely than.")

1. C > D > G
2. C > G > D
3. D > C > G

4. D > G > C
5. G > C > D
6. G > D > C

Which of these was true for your ranking of the eight statements about Bill? Figure 1 shows a typical distribution of responses from my students.

Recall that C = "Bill is an accountant," D = "Bill plays jazz," and G = "Bill is an account who plays jazz." Almost all of my students reported that, among these three statements, it was most likely that Bill is an accountant. Sure, that's a little stereotypical about accountants, but I'll buy that. Here's where things get weird: Half of my students thought it was more likely that Bill is a jazz-playing accountant than Bill plays jazz. That is, they reported the more specific outcome (jazz + accountant) as more likely than the more general outcome (jazz). That can't be!

Why not? Let's imagine we assembled all the people in the world who fit Bill's description in one room. For easy math, let's assume there are 100 such people. We ask all the Bills who play jazz to raise their hands. Suppose 20 of them do. That means there's a 20 percent chance that the more general outcome (jazz) is true. Next, we ask all the Bills who play jazz *and* are accountants to raise their hands. None of the other 80 Bills put their hands up, because none of them play jazz. Of the 20 jazz-playing Bills, maybe 17 of them put their hands down, since they aren't accountants. That leaves 3 jazz-playing, number-crunching Bills. That means there's a 3 percent chance that the more specific outcome (jazz + accountant) is true. I've made up numbers here, but regardless of the actual jobs and hobbies of the Bills of this world, that more specific probability (jazz + accountant) has to be less than the more general probability (jazz).

Here's another way to think about it (without numbers): If you were to bet twenty dollars on something, would you rather bet that Bill plays jazz, or that Bill plays jazz and is an accountant? If you bet on the latter, and Bill turned out to be a jazz-playing dentist, you would regret your bet. The more general outcome is just more likely than the more specific outcome.

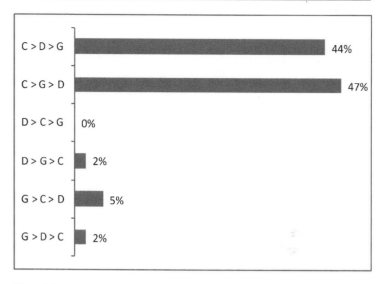

Figure 1. Summary of student responses to polling question about Bill the accountant.

Half of my students made the wrong bet. Why do so many people rank the probability of these statements incorrectly? Likely because we find the more specific outcome (jazz + accountant) more descriptive or useful than the more general outcome (jazz). This is an example of the *conjunction fallacy*, identified by Nobel Prize–winning economist and psychologist Daniel Kahneman in his book *Thinking, Fast and Slow*.[3] It's really common, and it gets in the way of the kind of probability modeling that my students need to do in my stats course.

During class, after the students have responded to the polling question and we've looked at the bar graph together, I ask a few students to talk through their reasoning. I point out that not all accountants are as dull as Bill seems to be (my dad, for instance, was a lot of fun), and then I explain the conjunction fallacy and how it applies to this problem, usually with a Venn diagram to supplement the room-full-of-Bills explanation I shared above. The students struggle a little with the explanation, but they all want to hear it. Why? Because through this sequence of technology-assisted activities, I have created a time for telling.

The technology is key here. First, the students need a chance to think about and respond to the multiple-choice question about their rankings independently. If I just asked for volunteers to respond, some students would, but other students would likely just wait and see what their more vocal peers said. For this classroom experiment to work, I need all the students to participate and to participate on their own, without being influenced by their peers. Second, the classroom response system collects and displays the aggregated student responses. That's critical because for my students to realize there's something challenging going on, they need to see that the class is split between two alternatives. That bar graph provides the right kind of challenge to their mental models. It effectively says to my students, "Your mental model might not be right." And this prepares them to listen to and make sense of the explanation that follows.

Creating a time for telling isn't the only way to use a classroom response system, but it can be a very effective way. Consider the following example from a different discipline.

Carl and His Rhinoceros

Ed Cheng teaches a course on evidence at the Vanderbilt University law school.[4] He likes to create an active learning environment in his classroom, and he was an early adopter of classroom response systems. Although modern BYOD systems allow for a variety of free-response questions, including free text, numeric response, and clickable image questions, Cheng gets a lot of mileage out of old-fashioned, multiple-choice questions. He finds that the constrained structure of multiple-choice questions can help create times for telling.

Cheng participated in a working group on classroom response systems at the Vanderbilt Center for Teaching in 2016, and he shared a series of questions he used at the beginning of one week of class, to help students review material from the previous week. All of the questions involved a guy named Carl and his rhinoceros. The first one was fairly straightforward, as Cheng told me.

Carl keeps a pet rhinoceros within a double electrified fence. A severe storm knocks out power, and the frightened rhino breaks through the fence, rampaging through the neighborhood and ramming Jodi's car. In an action against Carl, Jodi may recover:

A. Full damages because Carl converted Jodi's property
B. Full damages because trespass to chattels only requires substantial damages
C. Full damages because the rhino is a wild animal
D. Nothing, because Carl was not negligent

The correct answer is C. I am not a lawyer, but I understand from Cheng that Carl is responsible for predictable damages resulting from keeping a wild animal—like the ramming of a car—even if Carl takes steps to prevent those damages. There's a clear, unambiguous legal framework to apply in this case. Cheng said that, happily, all of his students answered this question correctly. He had a couple of students share their legal reasoning with the class, and, satisfied that they had conveyed the correct reasoning, he moved on.

The second question was more difficult.

Same facts, though instead of ramming a car, the rhino runs through Jerry's yard, breaking all of the irrigation pipes underground. (Rhinos can weigh up to five thousand pounds, which is the weight of a large car). In a subsequent strict liability action for owning a wild animal, Jerry can recover:

A. Nothing, because the harm is not within the risk
B. Nothing, because Carl was not negligent
C. Both A and B
D. None of the above

The correct answer is C again. In this case, the wild animal rule arguably doesn't apply because the perceived danger of the rhino is from ramming and stampeding, not its weight causing subterranean damage. Carl's behavior is therefore judged under the regular rule, which asks if he took "reasonable care," and Carl did his part by keeping his pet behind a double electrified fence. Cheng's students didn't do well on this question. Only 6 percent selected the right answer, although 18 percent were half-correct in selecting choice A. This was a harder question for the students, but, like the first one, there's a single correct answer. Cheng had some students share their perspectives on the question, but then he told them that the most popular answer, choice D with 76 percent of the vote, was wrong.[5] That was Cheng's first time for telling. When his students realized that most of them had chosen incorrectly, they sat up and listened to his explanation of the hypothetical.

Cheng's third question was very different.

> *Carl keeps a pet rhinoceros within a double electrified fence near a large forest. Signs are posted throughout the fence warning passersby about the danger of electricity (and the rhino). On a dark, moonless night, Fran gets lost in the forest, and not noticing the fence, walks into it. Fran gets electrocuted. In action again Carl, she can recover:*
>
> A.   Nothing, because Carl owes no duty to a trespasser
> B.   Nothing, because Carl was not negligent
> C.   Full damages, because Carl was negligent

Cheng reported that his students were split on this question: 31 percent for A, 39 percent for B, and 31 percent for C. Again, he called on students to justify their choices, drawing on all the legal reasoning they could muster. There were solid legal arguments for all three choices, and Cheng's students felt stuck. It was a time for telling!

Here's the thing about this third question: It doesn't have a single correct answer. A good lawyer could argue any of the three positions.

Cheng had two main goals in asking his students this series of questions about Carl and his rhinoceros. One was that he wanted to see if his students could muster the appropriate legal arguments for the situations in the first two questions, as a matter of review of the previous week's materials. Where students fell short, he worked with them to correct and refine their legal reasoning. The second goal, however, was more subtle and more important. Cheng wanted his students to know that in some situations, there's a clear legal answer to a question, and in other cases, there's isn't. A good lawyer knows when there's room for interpretation and can make compelling arguments within that gray area.

This series of clicker questions, with two single-correct-answer questions followed by a no-correct-answer question, created a useful cognitive dissonance for Cheng's students. They were expecting a single correct answer for the third question and, in fact, many of them likely carried mental models that assumed that all legal situations had correct answers. When the bar graph on the classroom projector showed that the students were split on the third question and when Cheng told them that there was no correct answer, they were ready to hear his message about legal gray areas and the kinds of critical thinking that lawyers have to do.

Cheng's third question isn't a multiple-choice question you would put on a test. It's not meant for that kind of assessment. But that question, enhanced by a classroom response system and healthy class discussion, helped Cheng's students realize a limitation in their mental models of evidence, then start to fix that limitation.

"You'll Have to Get Out of Bed First"

Classroom response systems aren't the only technologies useful for creating times for telling. Alisha Karabinus, for instance, uses a number of games in her writing courses at Purdue University to help students recognize they have more to learn about writing and research. One of those games is *9:05*, a free, text-based online game designed by Adam Cadre in which the player controls a character who wakes up in an apartment with the phone ringing.[6] The game's story is revealed as the player types commands to their character, like "answer phone" and "open door," to navigate and explore the apartment. The game can take five minutes or thirty minutes depending on the choices the

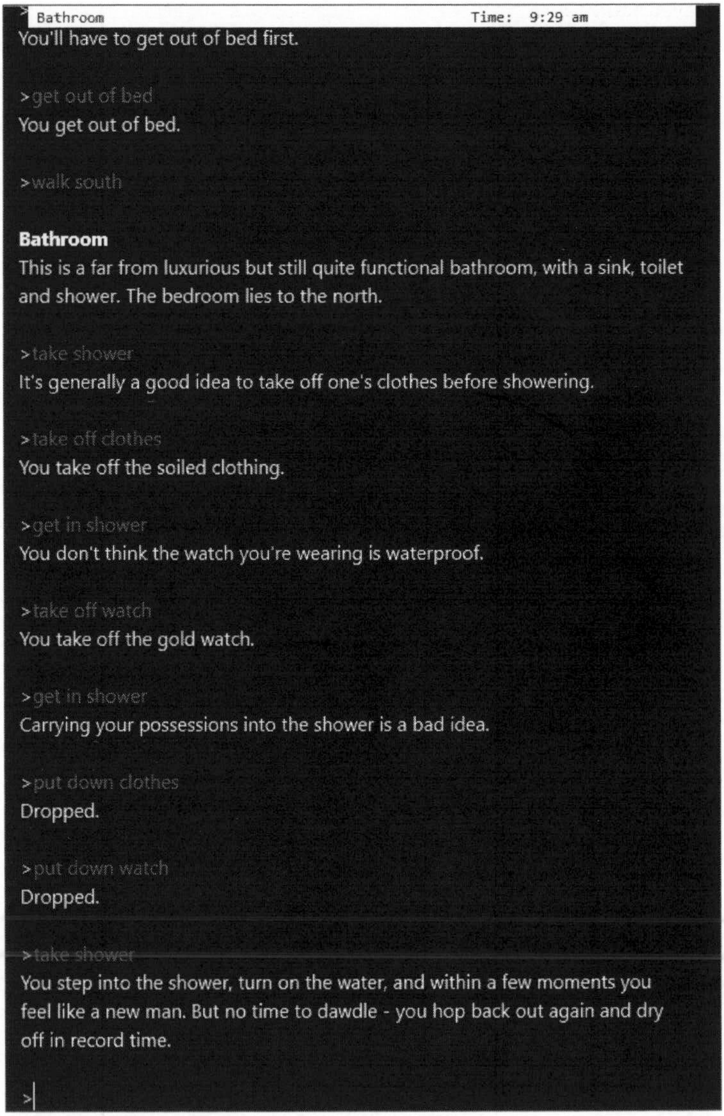

```
> Bathroom                                    Time:   9:29 am
You'll have to get out of bed first.

>get out of bed
You get out of bed.

>walk south

Bathroom
This is a far from luxurious but still quite functional bathroom, with a sink, toilet
and shower. The bedroom lies to the north.

>take shower
It's generally a good idea to take off one's clothes before showering.

>take off clothes
You take off the soiled clothing.

>get in shower
You don't think the watch you're wearing is waterproof.

>take off watch
You take off the gold watch.

>get in shower
Carrying your possessions into the shower is a bad idea.

>put down clothes
Dropped.

>put down watch
Dropped.

>take shower
You step into the shower, turn on the water, and within a few moments you
feel like a new man. But no time to dawdle - you hop back out again and dry
off in record time.

>|
```

Figure 2. Screenshot of the computer game *9:05* designed by Adam Cadre.

player makes, and there's a key plot point (no spoilers here!) that the player will discover sooner or later while playing that changes one's view of the game situation rather dramatically.

In spite of their technical majors, Karabinus's students aren't usually familiar with the interface for "old-school" text adventure games like *9:05*. They get frustrated trying to do simple things in the game, like taking a shower, which requires the character to take off their clothes and their watch, then put those items down before entering the shower (see fig. 2). Figuring out the right sequences of commands takes some work, with the game providing feedback that's both helpful ("You don't think the watch you're wearing is waterproof.") and not ("Verb error. The first word of your command was not recognized."). "I usually don't give them any help," Karabinus told me. "I just let them suffer and figure the game out on their own."

What does Karabinus use *9:05* to teach? "I use it to talk about transitions in their writing." I did not expect her to say that when I asked her that question. "I want them to get frustrated," she explained. "Then we talk about the frustration, and why it's so hard." Her students usually note that they don't think about all the steps it takes to, say, take a shower. That's because taking a shower is automatic to them. The game, however, requires them to be explicit about what they want their character to do. They can't omit something, assuming the game will fill in the gap. "This is what I want you to think about," Karabinus tells her students, "when you're writing your papers. Your thought process is invisible to me unless you tell me." Just as the game requires the player to be explicit, writing requires students to make explicit their thinking. The transitions students use between ideas in their writing should make clear the connections between those ideas.

Karabinus frames the conversation in terms of experts and novices. Students are novices when it comes to text adventure games, but they can't succeed at the game unless they develop some expertise with the interface. Someone with more experience playing these sorts of games is likely to discover that key plot point I mentioned early in the game, because they know how a game like this expects a player to explore the world it creates. Karabinus's students, however, often miss that plot point because they're novices. Karabinus wants her students to miss things in the game, to be frustrated or confused, because it gives them empathy for their future readers and motivates them to write more clearly and directly. And having the shared experience of playing the game provides Karabinus and her students a way to talk about this aspect of writing the rest of the semester.

Karabinus also has her students play the game *Her Story*, a video-based computer game by Sam Barlow.[7] In the game, the player is presented with a Windows computer desktop circa 1994 and uses the desktop interface to query a police database containing video clips of an interview with a woman about a murder. As the player tries different search terms in the database, they are presented with different video clips, helping them solve the murder mystery . . . maybe. Karabinus asks her students to play the game outside of class over a week, keeping a play log in which they track the search terms they use to explore the police database and respond to questions about the game both general and specific. The class discussion that week focuses on the game's story. It has an ambiguous ending, so the students make arguments about what happened concerning the murder using evidence from the game.

That discussion helps prepare students for future research papers involving arguments and evidence, but it also leverages the particular structure of *Her Story*. Depending on the search terms a player uses to query the in-game police database, players follow different paths through the game. As a result of the various paths the students take, they draw different conclusions about the ending of the game and argue for those conclusions using different evidence. Since each student's experience of the game is different, "some things have a lot more meaning for some students," Karabinus said, "and they really hang onto particular arguments." By asking students to track their search terms in their play logs, Karabinus helps her students understand why they arrive at different conclusions about the ending of the game. This collective experience prepares her students to make better use of search tools in their own research. "A slightly different phrasing can give you a hundred thousand different results in a library database," Karabinus said. For students used to simple Google searches, making good use of a library database requires a different mental model. Hearing their peers' *Her Story* search terms and how they led to different kinds of evidence shows the students the importance of using different search terms. "Having played *Her Story* together," Karabinus told me, "and seeing how that operates helps them make the connection faster."

"I love teaching with games," Karabinus said. "They get everyone excited or engaged or mad. They're all feeling something, and then they remember the experience." Through these and other games, Karabinus provides her students with experiences that confront them with their own limitations in writing and research. The game experiences create failure, and Karabinus leverages that failure. "That's what games really are. You fall in the hole, and then you realize you have to jump in a different place. You have to fail to progress." Karabinus uses that failure in the game environment to help students progress in their academic work.

Do Not Pass Go, Do Not Collect $200

The computer games *9:05* and *Her Story* are, perhaps, surprising choices for teaching students writing and research. In both games, it's the interface that Karabinus uses to create times for telling, not the content. However, as we saw with the Stanford BrainExplorer study, sometimes the content is what counts. Kimberly Rogers uses games in her sociology courses at Dartmouth, but her games function more like simulations given their relevance to her course topics. The games she uses, which are decidedly analog technologies, provide students with simulated experiences featuring notable points of failure that help them confront the limitations of their mental models.

For example, in Rogers's introductory sociology courses, she asks her students to play a modified version of the classic board game Monopoly. In the original game, players roll dice and move tokens around the board, generating income as they pass Go and buying real estate they can use to charge other players when they land on that property. The original game is, quite frankly, poorly designed. One's success in the game is almost entirely determined by luck; the only choice a player gets is whether to purchase a property they happen to land on. Rogers takes this game and ramps up the unfairness of it. When Rogers's students play the game, the token they select at the start of the game determines their starting assets—how much money they have and which properties they start the game owning—and their income when they make it around the board. That is, if they make it around the board. Because some players start with so little and others start with so much—including the high-rent properties of Boardwalk and Park Place for the wealthiest player—sometimes the poorest players don't even make it around to Go.

It's not until after her students finish playing this cruel version of Monopoly that Rogers reveals her secret: she scaled the starting assets and income in the game according to actual United Status Census data about income and wealth distribution. Each of the five tokens, with their unequal starting assets and income, represents a different wealth quintile according to census data. "It's a really striking moment for them," Rogers told me. There's something about playing through a game simulating wealth inequality that helps students pay attention to those inequalities and imagine their real-life impact. "It's one of the activities they most reference later in the class," Rogers said.

Rogers enhances this effect by not telling her students the rules of the game when they start playing. Some of her students know the basic rules of Monopoly and play in the usual fashion. Others, however, find themselves wanting to respond somehow to the unfairness of the situation. Some of the wealthier players create social programs in which they share their assets with the poorer players. Some students, perhaps having read a little Marx, stage a revolution and pool their assets. One player once proposed marriage to another player to get a step up in the game. These experiences, along with notes taken by students assigned to observer roles and an analysis of the economic mobility of players during the game (mostly downward, very little upward), fuel a rich discussion about wealth inequality in class the next day.

With "Stratified Monopoly," as Rogers calls it, an old game is given a tweak to create a time for telling. Later in the semester, Rogers uses a more complex game intentionally designed to teach. In RePlay Health, developed by the Dartmouth game design research lab Tiltfactor,

Figure 3. Kimberly Rogers' class playing RePlay Health. Photo by Adam Nemeroff.

teams of ten students work together to throw beanbags at targets for fake dollars, representing the productivity of their fictional town (fig. 3).[8] Each student is assigned a wallet that provides a health profile for the citizen they embody in the game, complete with health risk factors ("eats a healthy diet" or "abuses alcohol" or "lives in a high crime area"), health insurance status, and a health meter that ranges from green to yellow to red to black. (You don't want to be in the black.) Between beanbag tosses, event cards are drawn at random that affect players, usually for the worse, depending on the risk factors in their wallets. Citizens with unhealthy diets or those who don't get enough sleep or those who skip vaccines might get sicker. Players with unhealthier characters have to stand further away from the beanbag targets, making it harder for them to be productive. Players can visit healthcare providers to get better, but they have to skip a beanbag toss or two to do so, and the more effective healthcare providers require insurance.

Those basic mechanics would make for an interesting simulation, but it's the policy component of the game that really helps students understand how healthcare works. Every five rounds, teams are presented a choice of several healthcare policies to vote on and implement. Teams might pass a tobacco tax, effectively eliminating the smoking risk factor, or they might start a local farmer's market, giving all citizens healthy diets. Introducing community health workers, which provides another healthcare provider for citizens, is an option, as is universal healthcare. Players discuss their policy options, then vote, then move forward with another set of tosses and event cards under the new policy. Hopefully, the towns are more productive, but that's not always the case! After four policy votes and one final set of five beanbag tosses, the game ends. Players tally up their dollars and earn bonus points for being healthy, and the player with the most points wins.

RePlay Health may sound complicated, but students get the hang of it quickly. More importantly, the mechanics of the game model aspects of healthcare systems that Rogers wants her students to understand, including elements that are counterintuitive for students. Debriefing the game with students is essential. "One of the biggest aha moments this year," Rogers told me, "was when the students realized that the same person [character] had died in two different 'towns' from the same policy intervention." Both groups had implemented universal healthcare during their first policy vote. That sounded reasonable in theory, since it helped the most town members, but in each case the player with the most vulnerable wallet "died" before the second policy vote. "We know," Rogers said, "that policies that improve the health of vulnerable social groups more rapidly than the rest of the population tend to narrow health gaps faster." She told her students that during the pregame lecture on health disparities, but it wasn't until the postgame discussion, when students realized the same failure had occurred in two different towns, that Rogers's message hit home.

Who ended the game with good health or bad health? With high earnings or low earnings? What wallet characteristics seemed to have the biggest effect on health or productivity? Were the policy interventions effective? Were they more effective for some people than others? During the postgame discussion, Rogers helps her students analyze the ways race, class, gender, and other factors affect health and healthcare and how policy decisions can affect a large population of diverse people. "It's a lot easier," Rogers said, "for students to understand individual decision-making about their own health." Systems-level thinking is much harder, and there's some evidence that analog games like RePlay Health help students see the "big picture" more than digital games.[9] Also challenging for students is stepping outside of one's own experience and exercising the sociological imagination. Students who haven't had hard life experiences, like a lack of insurance or a serious health risk, sometimes have trouble connecting to the topic of health disparities. "And students who have actually experienced these things can be burdened to talk about their personal lives," Rogers said, "which is a vulnerable thing." RePlay Health acts as an equalizer, providing all students with a simulated experience they can discuss and learn from.

Rogers finds that helping students move past the limits of their own experience benefits from games and simulations that involve face-to-face player interaction. "There's something about game play with other people," Rogers told me, "that resonates on a level that's not possible when students engage the material on their own." In RePlay Health, for instance, players have to face the people who will be affected by their collective policy decisions. That player interaction is intentionally designed in a game like RePlay Health. It's a technology that creates a particular kind of experience for students, leading them to probe their prior understanding and to test their mental models. When designing her courses, Rogers looks for games that "create space for chaos, for the organic, emergent stuff that people do in a simulated environment. . . . The really cool stuff happens when people do their human thing in a context you've created for them."

Practical Advice

Creating times for telling for our students involves designing experiences that help them see and move past the limitations of their existing mental models. The success of this approach requires a careful match between the learning objective of the experience and the question, problem, or challenge posed to students. It also takes an intentional process, perhaps aided by technology, for guiding students through the experience and for helping them make sense of it. There's no one right way to design these "time for telling" experiences, but the following practical advice should help.

1. Look for common student misconceptions. Identifying these misconceptions can be challenging for a course you've not taught before, but sometimes you can find useful information about misconceptions in the literature on teaching and learning or by talking with colleagues. As you teach a course, however, you will inevitably discover problems in your students' mental models that make it hard for them to move forward in the course. I've often noticed patterns in student errors made in response to open-ended test questions, then turned those errors into wrong answers for in-class, multiple-choice questions of the kind described in this chapter.

2. Create experiences for your students that confront those misconceptions and incomplete understandings. Don't be afraid to give students a problem or challenge they can't quite meet and to let them get stuck. It's tempting to think that we need to give students the tools they need to work a problem before giving them the problem, but some productive failure can be highly motivational for students. Moreover, often the concepts or principles we want our students to learn can be fairly abstract. Grounding those ideas in a concrete example can help students make sense of them.

3. Know that changing mental models is hard work. We aren't inclined to rethink how we view the world unless we're confronted by the limitations of our existing mental models, but, even then, we humans tend to resist change. Sometimes it takes several experiences before students are willing to admit they don't understand something as well as they would like to think. And know that deeply embedded beliefs, especially ones that connect to a student's identity or politics or religion, aren't likely to change and can generate particularly

strong reactions. Choose your battles around such beliefs carefully.

4. Aim for questions that are hard, but not too hard. If you pose a challenge that all of your students can easily handle, you're probably not making good use of time. On the other hand, if you give students a task far beyond their abilities, they're likely to get more frustrated than motivated. There's often a Goldilocks zone where some students can make some progress on a challenge, or maybe a third or half of your students can answer a question correctly. Those are indications that you're likely to have a productive conversation with your students about the experience.

5. Tell your students that it's okay to struggle. Some of your students haven't experienced much failure in school and may see failure as a sign they don't have what it takes. Other students have failed plenty and see it as an indication they don't belong. Make sure your students know that learning involves failure. If they can see failure as an opportunity for growth, they're in a better position to persist and gain expertise.[10] Games and simulations can help. Taking students outside an academic domain and having a little fun can take the edge off the failure.

6. Talk it out. Discussion is key to helping students understand how their mental models work and move toward more robust frameworks. Ask students to explain their reasoning, both in small group discussions and full-class conversations. If students know that struggle is okay, they'll be more likely to share their reasoning, even if they're not sure they're correct. Consider *peer instruction* for a teaching structure modeled on the classic think-pair-share that works well with classroom response systems and times for telling.[11]

7. Wait for the right time to "tell." The time for telling is usually at the end of a sequence of activities. You may be tempted to jump in with explanations or correct a bit of poor reasoning expressed by a student during discussion, but the more heavy lifting your students can do to work through

the problem at hand, the better. They'll want to hear from you, however, eventually. Once students have surfaced most or all of the important connections, you can provide a clear, coherent explanation that summarizes and synthesizes the discussion.

8. Leverage the element of surprise. When Ed Cheng says to his students, "You're all correct" after that third question about Carl and his rhinoceros, that's a surprising moment for students. When students discover during their *Her Story* debrief that there's a major character in the game they may not have known about because they made different choices in the game, that underscores Alisha Karabinus's point about the importance of knowing your search interface. A moment of surprise can do a lot to engage students in learning.

9. Consider both independent experiences and group experiences. For the question about Bill the accountant, I need students to lock in their answers before hearing what their peers think to create my time for telling. Similarly, Alisha Karabinus wants her students to have different experiences playing *Her Story* so they can compare and contrast those experiences during class. On the other hand, Kimberly Rogers wants her students to work through her simulations with each other in order to help them understand the social dynamics at play. Be intentional about how you have students work together or not.

10. Look for technologies that are designed for learning. That includes technologies like classroom response systems and simulations like RePlay Health intended for educational use as well as technologies not created for classrooms that involve particular forms of learning. Games both digital and analog are often full of learning moments, in part because games are more fun when they are in that Goldilocks zone of being hard, but not too hard. Consider games whose content is on topic for your course but also those off topic if the mechanics or interface of the game might create a time for telling.

CHAPTER 2

Practice and Feedback

I LEARNED to ski in 2017. It wasn't pretty. The first day on the slopes, my instructor tried to convince me that if I put my skis in a wedge shape (the "pizza") with the tip of the wedge pointing downhill, I could control my descent. What she didn't say is that slowing oneself via the pizza also requires about ten different muscle groups in the legs and hips to do exactly the right thing in coordination. For the entire first day, the only way I could stop myself was falling down. I fell down. A lot.

By day two, however, I had figured out the wedge and was able to make it down the easiest slope on the mountain very slowly and generally without falling. However, I quickly learned that descent via the pizza is probably the most exhausting way to get down a mountain on skis. All those muscle groups have to activate the whole way down. By the end of the day, I was exhausted. I couldn't remember having been more tired, and I've run half marathons.

I took the morning of day three off.

After a few hours rest, my legs weren't quite the sacks of jelly they were the night before, so I hit the slopes again. I was determined to supplement my pizza technique with the French fry—keeping the skis parallel while going down the mountain side to side. Thanks to some advice from an experienced skier, I got the hang of it, but not without some more tumbles. My body was used to running, which gave me some endurance but also taught me to keep my limbs symmetric and parallel. Skiing, I found out, is all about asymmetry, about leaning and putting weight in one direction or the other. Making turns while French-frying took some figuring out.

Day four? Day four, I actually had fun! I could get down the easy slope at a pretty good pace, French-frying back and forth, and using the pizza to slow down when necessary. The hardest part of the fourth day was actually getting used to going fast. I'm not sure I've ever moved as quickly without some kind of motorized vehicle around me. That was exhilarating, but it meant having a little faith in myself that, as fast as I was going, I could slow myself down when the time came. I learned to trust myself and the two or three things I had figured out about skiing.

In fact, I felt confident enough late in the day to try a tree trail. That meant venturing just a little off the easy slope through the trees that lined it, following trails marked out by hundreds of past skiers. I fell down a few more times, since the turns were sharper than the ones I had to make on the slope. But I had a good guide who was patient and encouraging when I fell down and picked myself up again. (He was five years old.) And I felt great that I had done something outside my comfort zone and succeeded at it.

For me, learning how to ski involved lots of falling down and getting back up. Every time I fell, my body learned a little bit about what it takes to stay up and keep moving. That's how we develop our physical skills. We practice new skills, and we get feedback on that practice, sometimes from our bodies, sometimes from hard, immovable objects, like the ground. You can't learn to ski by sitting at the lodge watching other people ski—you have to hit the slopes and try it out yourself. Cognitive skills aren't entirely like physical skills, but in this regard, they're the same: you need practice and feedback to learn.

PRINCIPLE 2. *To learn new skills, students need practice applying those skills and to receive feedback on that practice.*

There's plenty of research pointing to the critical role of practice and feedback in learning—see *How Learning Works* by Susan Ambrose and colleagues[1] for a summary—but most of us understand this intuitively. That's why it's a little strange the college classroom sometimes acts as if practice and feedback aren't that important. Consider a traditional physics class. Students are introduced to new concepts and techniques during class via lecture, then go home and work problem sets to make sense of that new material. That is, they're practicing their learning after class, on their own or, if they're wise and the instructor allows it, in small groups. We know how important practice and feedback is to learning. Why not bring that into the classroom, when everyone is in the same place and available to help the process?

That's the primary motivation for many who practice the *flipped classroom*. They move introductory material from in-class lectures to pre-class readings and videos to make more class time available for practice and feedback. Instead of having students practice their new skills when they're on their own, instructors using this flipped approach acknowledge the centrality of practice and feedback to the learning process, then move that hard stuff from the individual space to the group space.[2] Although some disciplines, especially those in the humanities, have long structured learning experiences this way, the flipped approach represents a distinct shift in practice for many instructors. And there are even humanities faculty who use it creatively.[3]

As you think about ways to build practice and feedback into your class sessions, you might have to get a little creative to make time and space for this important part of learning. Technology can help with making that time and space available, through online videos or collaboratively annotated textbooks, and it can help provide practice opportunities outside of class (consider online homework systems, especially those that are built on adaptive learning systems), but technology can also provide direct opportunities for students to practice what they're learning during class and to receive feedback from peers and instructors on that practice. That's the kind of technology use that can be seen in the examples that follow.

In-Class Blogging

I used to call Humberto Garcia the "blogfather of the English department."

I met Garcia several years ago when he was an assistant professor of English at Vanderbilt. He was toying with the idea of using a course blog as a space for his students to write about the readings each week in one of his literature courses. We met, I gave him a crash course in WordPress, a free and commonly used blogging software, then he was off and running. Instead of asking his students to submit weekly reader response papers at the start of class, he asked them to share their reflections on the week's texts on the course blog, for all the students in the course to see. He found that they wrote better because they had an audience for their responses beyond their instructor. And he found that class discussions were richer because students came to class with ideas they wanted to talk about—their own and their peers'.

That was Garcia's first foray into course blogs, but not his last. In every subsequent semester, he would try out some new assignment or WordPress feature. He never took on too much at once; he knew he only had so much time to learn new tools or develop new assignments. But over time, he developed quite a variety of ways to use course blogs. I started taking notes from him on how to teach with blogs, and that's when I gave him the "blogfather" title. Other faculty members in Garcia's department had taught with blogs, but I was consistently amazed at the creative way he integrated blogging with class discussions.

Garcia teaches at the University of California–Merced now, where he continues to use blogs in innovative and intentional ways, often targeting specific skills he wants his students to practice. A typical weekly blogging assignment asks each student to write 200 to 350 words about the week's reading, either responding to a specific question about the reading or completing a creative writing exercise. In these blog posts, Garcia asks his students to be original and to take "calculated risks in providing interpretations that take us in new directions in our discussion," he told me recently.[4] He finds that this kind of prompt leads to better classroom discussions and that connecting the pre-class blogging assignment and the in-class discussions is key. "It's absolutely essential," Garcia said, "that you integrate what's going on outside the class with blogging with what's going on inside the class."

That integration can take different forms. Sometimes Garcia simply picks a great student blog post, one that brings a novel idea or a good question, and shares it at the start of class, using it as a launch point for class discussion. Other times, usually after building some rapport in the classroom, Garcia will select a handful of blog posts from students who won't mind a little critique and ask students to work in groups to evaluate and even grade those posts. If it's too early in the semester for that, he might select some student blog posts from a previous offering of the course for students to discuss and dissect. One of the advantages of a course blog is that it makes student work public and persistent in a way that student discussion posts in a course management system are not. This makes it easy to direct students to writing from previous semesters.

One of the more unexpected methods Garcia uses to integrate pre-class writing and in-class discussions is through *in-class blogging*. I call this unexpected because it's rare in my experience for instructors to ask students to blog during class. However, Garcia has found this to be a very effective way to develop their critical thinking skills and to set the stage for an engaging class discussion. He asks students to select their favorite peer blog post, then leave a three-to-five-sentence comment on that post responding to the following prompt: "What is the most original idea presented in this blog post, and how can it be enhanced or improved?"

Not only does this activity motivate his students to take their peers' writing more seriously (and thus appreciate the audience they have for their own writing), but the prompt pushes them to think more critically about the ideas they are encountering and writing about. Garcia wants his students to come up with their own takes on the texts they study and to share those perspectives in persuasive ways. By asking his students to evaluate and respond to each other's posts, he gives them the chance to practice these intellectual moves. And by having them do this work in class, he opens up opportunities for students to receive feedback on this practice, either as their ideas weave into the subsequent class discussion or, more directly, when Garcia selects a few posts and comments to show on the big screen and discuss with his students.

I love this idea of asking students to practice making a particular intellectual move during class through the course blog. I've used it myself in the cryptography seminar I teach. One semester, I asked my students to read the section in the textbook that discusses the success of Alan Turing and the other Bletchley Park codebreakers in defeating the German Enigma machine during World War II, then to make an argument in a blog post about why the British were more successful in the cryptography war than the Germans. During class, I asked students to select a peer's blog post and leave a comment that builds on its argument somehow, adding some kind of nuance or complexity, or arguing against it in some compelling way. These moves—adding complexity, countering an argument—are the moves my students will need to make in the argumentative writing they'll do in my course and later in college. I think it's a great use of class time to have them practice those moves, then to bring up a few examples on the big screen to discuss with the entire class. I can point out, for instance, when a student added an example to a peer's argument but didn't add any nuance to the argument through the example. My feedback helps one student directly and all the students indirectly as they reflect on their own blog comments.

Humberto Garcia has explicit learning goals for his students, ways of approaching the study of literature he wants them to cultivate and develop. And he has found a useful tool for helping them practice those skills during class. There are other ways to go about this, of course, but given the many ways Garcia uses his course blog, it's an easy reach for him to ask his students to use it for these in-class activities. And the public, persistent nature of the course blog helps his students see more value in their own writing and that of their peers.

Seeing a New Role

Vanderbilt teacher educator Elizabeth Self got the idea while pretending to be sick for her husband.

Self's husband was in medical school, studying to be a doctor. Part of that education involved *standardized patient encounters*, in which medical students practice their diagnostic skills and bedside manners with actors playing the role of patients. Self would help her husband get ready for these encounters by pretending to be sick, giving him a chance to, say, rehearse the steps for a neurological exam. Self was teaching school at the time, having completed her teacher training a few years earlier, and wondered if this kind of simulation was used in teacher education. Could preservice teachers work with actors taking on the roles of students, parents, or administrators to practice the kind of interpersonal communication they would need once in school settings? Yes, as it turns out, although it took Self a few years—and a return to school herself to get a PhD from Vanderbilt University—to answer this question. Today, Self designs, implements, and assesses clinical simulations for preservice teachers, simulations that are enhanced in intentional ways by technology.

Recall a challenging encounter you had with a student or fellow teacher or an administrator, perhaps in an office or in the hallway outside a classroom. Ever wish you could go back to that moment, rewind it and play it in slow motion, maybe hit pause so you could rethink how you handled the situation? That's the kind of experience Self creates for her preservice teachers. She works with actors to create scenarios that reflect the kind of challenging encounters teachers sometimes (or often) have in their work. The preservice teacher receives some basic information about the scenario—where it takes place, who the other party is, what's happening at this point in the school year. The actor receives much more detailed information about the student, parent, or school staff member they are portraying, their background and motivations and concerns. The preservice teacher and the actor sit down together in a mock classroom, and the simulation begins. Depending on what choices and moves the preservice teacher makes, the actor reacts as necessary, responding as their character would using a prescribed set of responses.

The simulation itself is a valuable opportunity for future teachers to practice the kinds of communication skills they'll need in school settings. But the simulation is just the beginning of the learning opportunity. The encounter is filmed, and the preservice teacher is asked to review the video and reflect on the encounter. This ability to see themselves (via video) as future students, parents, and coworkers will see them can be transformative for preservice teachers. "They're getting to see what they look like sitting as the person in authority," Self said, "after having been out of the high school situation for only a year or two. For a lot of them, it's a moment of transition to sit around at the other side of the desk, so to speak, and to figure out who they are in that role."[5] The video provides an opportunity for a form of self-feedback that's useful to Self's students.

The reflection goes even deeper, however, as students are prompted to think critically about the scenario in which they participated. What assumptions did you have coming in? Were they met? If not, why not? What kinds of questions did you ask? What kind of information did those questions elicit? These prompts help students unpack their own experiences and expectations. Indeed, many of Self's students are planning careers in urban school districts, and the scenarios require the preservice teachers to encounter issues of difference and power they find challenging, perhaps a case where a student feels singled out because of her race or a parent-teacher conference with an immigrant parent.[6]

Some students might expect Self to provide some kind of script to follow in these kinds of situations. However, that's not her goal. Self wants her students to understand that they can't prepare for every possible situation or encounter, that their response in hard moments will need to take into consideration the details and context and, most importantly, the humans involved. Self encourages her preservice teachers to set aside their assumptions about what a teacher should do in a situation and to connect with the person on the other side of the table as a human. "Part of our work," she said, "is disrupting hegemonic forms of teaching that have not served students well, particularly students who have been marginalized in society."[7]

When students come to such realizations, however, varies considerably. In her research, Self studies the timing of critical learning moments for future teachers during this process. They don't often have a lightbulb moment in the minutes after the simulation, when they're asked to do a raw debrief by themselves, just speaking into an iPad camera. Sometimes it happens in the following week, when they watch themselves on video and reflect. Sometimes it happens in the group debrief with other preservice teachers in the next class session. Sometimes it doesn't happen until the last class of the semester, when a stray comment from a peer connects with an earlier experience in a profound way. Sometimes it takes years for teachers to realize that there's more going on in the interactions they have with students and others than it seems on the surface. The sooner teachers can have a deeper understanding of the dynamics of difference and power they encounter, the better. The clinical simulations provide a safe opportunity for that, with trained actors instead of actual students. "A big part of my goal was to create a way for teachers to learn these things," said Self, "in a way that minimized harm to some of our most vulnerable students."[8]

The technology Self uses in the clinical simulations is conceptually simple—video capture with good audio—but it is critical to provide her students with the opportunity to practice being teachers and, perhaps more importantly, to see themselves as teachers.

Engineering In-Class Group Work

Richard Flagan had an opportunity that turned into a problem. A revision to the chemical engineering curriculum at the California Institute of Technology, where Flagan teaches, made possible a new course on using programming techniques to solve engineering problems. Flagan's engineering students needed to know how to use tools like MATLAB to run statistical analyses on what he calls "monster" data sets. The computer science courses his students took didn't quite provide this skillset, and the new course would give Flagan the chance to teach these skills directly to chemical engineering majors, preparing them for future courses.

The problem was that, after walking through various programming tasks during class on the big screen, Flagan found that his students kept getting stymied by the particularities of the MATLAB programming language on assignments. They seemed to follow during class, even pulling out their laptops and coding along with what they saw on the projector screen. But when they were on their own, after class, they would get stuck on fairly simple things, like the use of punctuation in MATLAB syntax or passing parameters to functions. Flagan needed a way to discover during class the kinds of problems his students would have learning MATLAB, so he could address those hang-ups preemptively. He wanted to move his students' practice into the shared classroom space, so he could provide more timely feedback on that practice.

Flagan talked to Cassandra Volpe Horii, director of the Center for Teaching, Learning, and Outreach at Caltech. She observed Flagan's class and suggested a piece of relatively simple technology that led to a transformation in Flagan's teaching: mini projectors. Her teaching center was able to provide Flagan with a set of these small projectors, each about the size of a paperback novel. The mini projectors enabled him to ask his students to work on programming problems during class in groups of four. Flagan's course met in a traditional lecture hall, with fixed rows of tiered seats, so group work wasn't easy. But the classroom walls were white, which meant each group could point its mini projector at a nearby wall and collaborate on the coding task at hand.

As the groups worked, Flagan would circulate among them, looking at what they projected and listening to their questions. "I got a far better sense of where students were having difficulty," Flagan told me, "from being in the room, seeing them work through the problems." By hearing them talk and watching them code, Flagan was able to catch and address their errors and misconceptions, either directly to a student group or through mini lectures to the entire class. After class, students would have further opportunities to practice, as they worked through problems that were extensions of the ones they tackled during class.

Flagan's students weren't used to this kind of group work. They reported to him that most of their computer science courses had strong prohibitions in place about seeing another student's code. Flagan, however, was asking students to write code together. Some students would try to tackle the in-class programming challenges individually, but they would invariably get stuck and end up turning to their group members for help. By talking through the problems and by coding together on the shared laptop, students would figure out solutions to easier challenges, then bring harder ones to Flagan for assistance.

The mini projectors facilitated a certain kind of collaborative work that would have been nearly impossible without them in the lecture hall where Flagan's course met. And that collaborative work provided Flagan's students with just the kind of practice and feedback (from their peers and from their instructor) that they needed to learn the programming skills Flagan's course targeted. Purchasing mini projectors to transform a lecture hall isn't something that most instructors can do, but a department, school, or teaching center budget might be able to handle this level of technology investment. It's certainly cheaper than renovating a classroom, and in Flagan's case, it was just enough technology to help him start a process of transforming his teaching. He saw enough value in his experimental small-group approach to using class time that he arranged for the next offering of the course to be held in a classroom that better supported group work, one with tables where students could more easily collaborate around a laptop. The new classroom let Flagan further transform his teaching so that group programming activities became a regular part of the course instead of something his students did only occasionally. And having made this fairly substantial change to his teaching, Flagan is excited to tweak and tinker with his approach in future semesters, just as you would expect from an engineer.

Close Reading, Slow Reading

Historians work with primary sources—the letters, journals, ledgers, and other documents created by particular people living in particular times and places. Working with primary sources requires historians to immerse themselves in these documents, reading them carefully line by line to try to understand every person, place, thing, and idea mentioned in them. This approach to primary sources is what some call *close reading*, and Wheaton College historian Kathryn Tomasek knows that her students (historians in training) struggle with close reading. "One of the things that is always challenging," she said, "is to help students understand the necessity of spending time with your sources and becoming immersed in them."[9]

Back in 2004 Tomasek learned about a set of technologies that she has found very useful in helping students develop close reading skills. That summer, she attended a workshop taught by faculty from the Women Writers Project at Brown University on TEI, the Text Encoding Initiative. TEI is an effort by academics to develop a way to annotate, or *mark up* (in the parlance of TEI), digital versions of documents, describing the content of the documents in ways that are readable by both humans and computers.[10] For instance, consider this entry from Eliza Wheaton's 1862 travel journal:

Wednesday 16th

Drizzly morng.

at 9, o'clk. we left in carriage for East Boston where we found the Steam Ship Niagara laying at her wharf taking in freight +c. Soon friends met us on board—among whom was Cousin Wm. Chapin + Saml. also Bro Judson Chapin, Missy Mitchell King, Carpenter, Church, Gorge Wild, Con. and Mr and Mrs Beane—The last two had but a few moments before the Bell called all to leave the ship who were not outward bound passengers . . . The last farewells had to be given—These last expressions of friendship touched my heart and with deep emotion I parted with them—God only knows whether ever to look on their faces again or no on Earth.

This text is already more human- and machine-readable than the original, handwritten journal entry, as it has been transcribed to digital text. However, as it is, computers can't do much with this text, since it's all one big string of letters and numbers and characters, as far as a computer can see it. That's where TEI comes in. Here's a marked-up version of the same entry, using the TEI guidelines:

```
<div type="entry">

<opener>

<dateline><date      cert="high"      when="1862-04-16">Wednesday
16<choice><orig>"</orig><reg>th</reg></choice></date></
dateline>

Drizzly morng.

</opener>

<p>
```

```
at 9, o'clk. we left in carriage for <name type="place">East
Boston</name> where we found the <name type="orgTransport">Steam
Ship Niagara</name> laying at her wharf taking in freight
+c. Soon friends met us on board—<pb n="2" rend="2
supralinear D"/>among whom was <name type="person">Cousin
Wm. Chapin</name> + <name type="person">Saml.</name> also
<name type="person" key="ebwdiaJC">Bro Judson Chapin</
name>, <name type="person">Missy Mitchell King</name>, <name
type="person">Carpenter</name>, <name type="person">Church</
name>, <name type="person" key="ebwdiaGW">Gorge Wild</
name>, Con. and <name type="person" key="ebwdiaEKB"><!—
need to tag Mr. Beane—>Mr and Mrs Beane</name>—The last
two had but a few moments before the Bell called all to
leave the ship who were not outward bound passengers . . .
The last farewells had to be given—These last expressions of
friendship touched my heart and with deep emotion I parted
```

with them—God only knows whether ever to look on their faces
again or no on<!—meant to be "me on"—> Earth.

</p>

[11]

If all those angle brackets are intimidating, please don't stop
reading! We can figure this out together. Those words between angle
brackets are tags, and they come in pairs, describing for both humans
and computers what lies within the pairs. For instance, <p> marks the
beginning of a paragraph, and its mate </p> marks the end of that
paragraph. The tags <dateline> and </dateline> mark the start and
end of the date part of the journal entry. Notice with the <name> tag,
there's an associated attribute that describes the type of name being
tagged. For example, <name type="place"> tells us that East Boston
is a place name, and <name type="person"> tells us that Cousin Wm.
Chapin is a person's name.

Thanks to that 2004 workshop on TEI and in collaboration with
Wheaton College librarians and archivists, Tomasek asked her history students to mark up historical documents drawn from Wheaton
College's special collections. They started by transcribing and marking
up the journal of Maria E. Wood, music teacher and daughter of a
Baptist minister who wrote about her life just after the American
Civil War. Tomasek's students had to read the journal entries carefully
and intentionally to identify and interpret (via TEI tags) the people,
places, and course themes, including family, work, religion, death, and
mourning, present in the entries. This process required students to
practice the kind of close reading skills that Tomasek wanted them to
develop, and she spent class time having them engage in transcription
and markup collaboratively (a good projector system helped), so that
her students could receive feedback on their work as they went along.
As an added benefit, Tomasek said, "Student loved it. They felt like
they got to know Maria Wood, and to really care about her life. They
really wanted to know what happened in her life after the period of
the journal, which I consider to be a real success."[12]

In subsequent years, Tomasek, her library collaborators, and her students transcribed and marked up diaries and journals from Eliza B. Wheaton, founder of Wheaton Female Seminary; ephemera from Wheaton's 1862 trip to Europe with her husband, Laban Morey Wheaton, and his business partner David E. Holman; and financial transactions found in Laban Wheaton's daybooks from 1828 to 1859. The latter documents required a different approach to close reading and markup, given the quantitative nature of the daybook entries. Some of this work took place in Tomasek's courses, some outside of courses through undergraduate research experiences, and some in cemeteries, as students explored the town of Norton, Massachusetts, to find birth and death dates of people mentioned in the documents! The text encoding assignment has enabled Tomasek's students to "do history" by giving them the chance to practice the skills historians use to make sense of primary sources.[13]

Table for Nine

There are active learning classrooms, and then there are Active Learning Classrooms. Cornelia Lang, associate professor of physics and astronomy at the University of Iowa, used to teach large intro astronomy courses that featured lots of active learning—think-pair-share activities, clicker questions, quiz competitions in the style of *Who Wants to Be a Millionaire*, and more. She gave her students far more to do during class than just listen and taken notes, even though she taught in a lecture hall that didn't make active learning easy. So when the university made available a new classroom that was custom built for active learning, Lang jumped at the chance to teach there.

Today, Lang teaches regularly in one of the TILE classrooms at the University of Iowa. TILE stands for Transform, Interact, Learn, and Engage, and these classrooms are part of a trend in classroom design called *active learning classrooms*.[14] These classrooms, like the ones at Iowa, feature flat floors (not tiered or stadium seating), tables and chairs intended for students to face each other and work in groups, lots of whiteboards or other marking surfaces, good Wi-Fi for students to bring and use their laptops, and typically a variety of audio-visual projection and amplification systems so that anyone in the room can present to everyone else in the room. Where a traditional lecture hall makes it challenging to adopt active learning instruction, an active learning classroom has multiple affordances that make these pedagogies easier to implement.[15]

Lang teaches a "Big Ideas" general education course called "Life in the Universe" in a TILE active learning classroom. She teaches the course with two faculty colleagues, one from biology and one from geoscience. It's a true team-taught course, where each class session is designed and facilitated by multiple instructors—not the tag-team approach to team teaching used in some courses. It's a fairly large course, with eighty students interacting with each other around tables, nine students per table. Every class features group activities at those tables, sometimes involving the entire table, sometimes in groups of three, and sometimes a mix. (Lang says that she and her coteachers have gotten very good at multiplying and dividing by three and nine.) Understanding life in the universe is a hard topic, and it requires an interdisciplinary approach. Lang and her colleagues know that it's not enough for students to hear about the topic from different disciplinary perspectives. The students need to engage in that clash of disciplines firsthand, which is why every class is built around interdisciplinary group activities.

For example, one class session focuses on extreme forms of life. The class starts with brief lectures from Lang and one of her colleagues, no more than five or ten minutes each. The biologist shares some information about metabolism and energy; Lang gives some examples of organisms (bacteria and so on) found in extreme places here on Earth. Then students move into the group activity, which asks them to match extreme organisms from Earth to the kinds of environments around the solar system where they might survive or thrive. Each table is assigned a different environment (say, Enceladus, the sixth-largest moon of Saturn), and the students at that table work in teams of three to research different aspects of that environment, drawing on their readings as well as various websites the instructors have recommended.

The whole class is working a list of extremophiles, and each table's task is to determine which organism from this list would do best in the environment that table's students have been assigned, based on the research they do together. There's a list of environments on the document camera in the middle of the room, visible to the whole room through multiple projection screens. When a table thinks it's got a match, it sends a runner up to write in the chosen extremophile next to the assigned moon or planet. When all the teams are done (or time is up, whichever comes first), the teams take turns presenting their cases to the whole class, projecting a laptop screen or drawing a picture on the document camera or using a nearby microphone as needed to share their arguments for the extremophile-environment match they've determined. Instructors and fellow students ask questions of each team, giving them a chance to correct or clarify or expand on their reasoning.

Lang's classroom has a lot of technology in it, from the moveable chairs to the round tables to the whiteboards and TV screens for every team to the four projector screens scattered around the room. She and her colleagues have learned to use this technology fluidly to support student activities. They might send activity instructions to the table TVs while projecting a series of images on the big screens and keeping a running checklist on the document camera. Given the topic of the course, they have students put things in sequential order a lot, so they might have a list or set of images to order on the table TVs while students use their whiteboards to draft their sequences and the big screens display a list of teams who have finished the activity. Lang and colleagues also use a lot of timelines, timelines that cover very large ranges of time. (Very large.) They'll run a timeline across multiple whiteboards around the periphery of the room, using it as a touchpoint with the students throughout class.

As technology rich as many of Lang's activities are, the goal of the activities is to help the students grapple with the information, principles, and skills it takes to understand life in the universe. Sometimes that goal means laptops out, internet on. Other times, the laptops go away, and students spend time brainstorming at whiteboards. The technology is used in ways that support the pedagogical goals. Lang is transparent with her students about this. "We thought that they would figure it out," Lang said, "that we're using all these different strategies [intentionally]. We found it better to actually just say it. 'Today, we're doing X, Y, and Z, because that's what the task requires.'

That helps them realize that there are many ways that they can learn in that room, from us, and from each other."[16]

Lang's role as instructor shifts when she teaches in an active learning classroom. She might lecture for a few minutes at the start of class, but most of class time is spent circulating among the students, asking them questions, directing them to resources for their questions, and prodding them to go deeper with the material. Instructors can try to interact with students like this in traditional lecture halls, but active learning classrooms can make it easier to do so.[17] Lang finds this kind of interaction with students personally fulfilling. Her science colleagues do, too. Many of them request to teach in classrooms that allow for this kind of interaction, classrooms with tables and moveable chairs and lots of whiteboards, even if they don't have the higher-end technologies of a TILE classroom. Students benefit from this kind of class structure and instructor interaction because it provides lots of opportunities for practice and feedback. Lang sees this as a question of equity. "Strong students are going to do well in almost any environment you put them in," Lang said. "The students who probably need us the most are the ones who can benefit the most from these times when you are walking amongst them."

All-Skate

When I was in middle school, the thing to do was to go roller skating. I was never very good at it, but when all the other thirteen-year-olds are spending Friday night at the skate center, that's what you do. Picture a young man, tall and slim, moving gingerly around the hardwood, occasionally retreating to the safety of the carpeted areas along the walls. That was me. Once or twice a night the DJ would announce that it was time for the hokey pokey, inviting skaters to the middle of the hardwood to put their left foot in, put their left foot out, put their left foot in, shake it all about, then do the hokey pokey. I usually watched from afar because doing the hokey pokey required a little more coordination than I felt I possessed. Later, the DJ would let us all know that it was time for couples-skate. This was an opportunity for teenage skaters to hold the hands of their dates and . . . skate romantically? Is that possible? Regardless, this math team captain was usually flying solo, so he sat out couples-skate.

But after one of these activities, the DJ would put on a new song and come on the PA and announce, "This song is an all-skate." That was our cue that everyone was invited to skate. You didn't have to have a date, you didn't have to have particular talent, you just needed skates on your feet. Everyone was invited and encouraged to participate. And so I did.

All-skate. It's a metaphor I always keep in mind when I think about the kind of classroom environments that support practice and feedback, especially those that use technology. Consider how the instructors described in this chapter created all-skate environments, where every student was invited and encouraged to participate. Humberto Garcia asks each of his students to read and respond to a peer's blog post during class so that each student has the chance to give and receive feedback on their critical analyses of the week's text. In Elizabeth Self's preservice teacher courses, every student has the chance to take on the role of teacher during a clinical simulation, and every student is asked to reflect on the experience. Richard Flagan, the chemical engineering professor, started using small, portable projectors so that he could find out what roadblocks his students had with the material—not just a handful of students asking questions during lecture but all students through their small group work. Kathryn Tomasek, the digital historian, wanted all of her students to have the chance to practice their close reading, so she spent class time having them practice marking up documents using TEI. And Cornelia Lang structures class sessions in her active learning classroom intentionally with small group activities so that every student plays a role and is accountable for their contributions.

A few years ago, I read yet another opinion column titled "In Defense of the Lecture." As with other such essays, this one argued that the college lecture was, in spite of the research, a very effective form of teaching. Usually when I see these perspective pieces, two basic arguments are made: 1) lectures totally worked for me, so they should work for my students; 2) my lectures aren't dry, boring hours of exposition, they're engaging, full of questions and answers and back-and-forths with my students. I'm not convinced by either argument. Just because a particular teaching approach worked for you, that's no reason to believe it will work for the majority of your students. After all, we're the odd birds who pursued PhDs and other advanced degrees to go teach college. The vast majority of our students bring a different set of motivations, interests, and background experiences to the classroom. As for the second argument, if your lecture is full of lots of discussion with students, it's not really a lecture. In fact, in the essay that bugged me that day in 2015, the classroom the author described was full of active learning instruction. The author just thought of all small group activity, classwide discussion, and instructor-student interaction as "lecture."

The research that shows active learning instruction is more effective than traditional lecture uses a more precise definition of lecture. Consider the meta-analysis published in the *Proceedings of the National Academy of Sciences* a few years ago. The authors looked at 228 published studies comparing active learning instruction to traditional lecturing. Each study had a structure something like a control group study: two sections of the same course were taught, one using traditional lecture, the other using some form of active learning instruction. Each section used the same final exam or some other common assessment, allowing for the comparison of student success and student learning across the two sections. Of course, none of the 228 studies were true randomized control group studies—those are next-to-impossible in higher education—but all came close and had results that could be compared and aggregated. Selecting these studies, however, required a couple of key working definitions. *Active learning* was defined as "learning through activities and/or discussion in class . . . that emphasizes higher-order thinking and often involves group work," while *traditional lecture* was taken to be "continuous exposition by the teacher."[18]

The results of the meta-analysis by Freeman and colleagues were compelling: active learning instruction leads to greater student learning and student success than traditional lecture. The failure rates in the traditional lecture sections studied were, on average, 34 percent. Note that all the individual studies were in STEM fields, and most were large, introductory courses with traditionally high failure rates. In the active learning sections, the average failure rate was dramatically lower, only 22 percent. And final exam scores in the active learning sections were, on a one-hundred-point scale, an average of six points higher than those in the lecture sections. Carl Wieman, Nobel laureate and STEM education reformer, found these results such a convincing case for active learning instruction that he described lecturing as "the pedagogical equivalent of bloodletting."[19]

The research is pretty clear. What's less clear, as it happens, is what we mean when we say *lecture*. Freeman and colleagues used a fairly precise definition: "continuous exposition by the teacher." But colloquially, the term *lecture* often describes a host of teaching methods used by college and university instructors. I felt that some who were writing "In Defense of the Lecture" columns were talking right past the educational researchers telling them to stop lecture, and vice versa, so I wrote a blog post with a provocative title: "In Defense of Continuous Exposition by the Teacher."[20] I made the point that almost no one argues for continuous exposition by the teacher, and that if we did a little better job communicating, we might not have quite so many hot debates about the role of lectures in postsecondary education.

Of course, my blog post drew out a few commenters who wanted to defend the lecture, including some who even argued for the value of continuous exposition. And that brings us back to all-skate. In a comment on my post, Davidson College digital studies professor Mark Sample responded to those who defended continuous exposition: "One of the problems with lectures—and especially in the extreme form of 'continuous exposition by the teacher'—is that we *don't know* what's going on in students' heads during the exposition. So, yes, there's an opportunity for students to, as [the previous commenter] puts it, dismiss, take issue, agree, and make connections, but we *don't know* if that's what's going on."[21]

When we spend an entire class period lecturing, it's likely that a handful of students will respond to our questions, ask questions of their own, and generally show us through words and actions that they are engaged actively in making sense of the lecture material. But that's just a few students. What about the rest of them? When we plan activities that provide our students opportunities for practice and feed-back during class, we should structure those activities to include as many students as we can. That is, we should endeavor to create all-skate environments in our classrooms, ones where all students are invited and encouraged to participate in active learning. And the activities we plan should, ideally, make visible our students' learning so we get a better sense of how they're engaging with the material for the day. (I have much more to say on this idea of making learning visible in chapter 3.)

Technology is not necessary to create all-skate opportunities for practice and feedback, but it can often help, especially when class sizes are larger than we might prefer. Consider Humberto Garcia's use of student blog posts during class. In his smaller classes, Garcia will ask students to work in groups to read and evaluate another student's blog posts. That leads to healthy class discussion when student groups report out. In his larger classes, it's challenging to have groups of students evaluate many different peer blog posts, and the reporting-out process is more chaotic, too. In recent semesters, Garcia has started experimenting with the use of a classroom response system, like those described in the first chapter, to facilitate this kind of activity in his larger courses. He selects maybe three student blog posts on one theme and asks students to identify the blog post that they thought was the most effective interpretation of the text. He then asks students to submit their votes using a classroom response system. The system aggregates the responses and projects a bar chart on the screen at the front of the room. Garcia can quickly see how many of his students thought blog post 1 was best, how many thought 2 was best, and so on. He uses the bar chart to launch a structured whole-class discussion. He might start by saying, "It looks like almost half of you thought the second blog post was most compelling. Can someone who voted for number 2 share their reasons why?" He hears from several students sharing elements of that blog post they responded to. Then he'll move onto the other blog posts, each time asking students to share their perspectives.

Garcia notes that even when he gets fifty students blogging before class, "It's impossible for you to actually engage with fifty students directly in class." He wants the ideas his students generate through their blog posts to form the foundation of class discussion, and he wants all his students to interact with and think about those ideas. "A lot of key themes and ideas would emerge from the blog posts," said Garcia. "I would use that as a way to structure and develop clicker questions. That way, I was still engaging with their blog posts in a very mediated form," through the classroom response system. Garcia can't have fifty students participate actively in a whole-class discussion, but he can ask every student to read a few blog posts, select the one they think is strongest, and to discuss the blog posts in pairs or small groups. He's creating an all-skate environment, and he's using technology to provide a mechanism and a motivation for his students to participate. It's kind of like he's set up a hardwood floor and passed out roller skates. Students still have to put on the skates and get on the floor, but he's designed an environment where everyone can do that.

For another example, consider the following question from my Vanderbilt colleague Janice Law, who teaches ophthalmology residents. She presents the question alongside an optical scan of an eye.

> *Your patient is a sixty-four-year-old female with two months of blurred vision and 20/200 eyesight. Given the photo seen here, how would you treat?*
>
> A. Bevacizumab
> B. Vitrectomy with ILM peel
> C. Intravitreal jetrea
> D. Vitrectomy with ERM peel
> E. Intravitreal triesence

Like Ed Cheng's question about Carl and the rhinoceros in chapter 1, Law's multiple-choice question is an interesting one because it doesn't have a single correct answer. According to Law, more than one of the treatments listed is reasonable given the limited information available in the question. More than one of the treatments is a poor choice, too. This kind of diagnostic choice, selecting the best available option based on limited information, is something that her residents will have to face regularly in their work as doctors. Law builds in opportunities to practice this kind of diagnostic thinking in her class sessions, and she uses a classroom response system to facilitate those opportunities. Students vote using their response devices, and the bar chart generated by the system gives Law guidance in how to respond. If most of her students select the better answers, she can have a few students provide their rationales but fairly quickly move on, knowing that most of her students understand the situation. If, however, a number of her students select wrong answers, she can spend more time with the question, perhaps by asking students to talk about the question in pairs and vote again, or spending more time in whole-class discussion about the question.

The point of a question like this isn't to get the right answer. There isn't a right answer, at least not a single one. The point is to practice the kind of critical reasoning and ways of working with evidence that ophthalmologists need. The multiple-choice format of the question makes the interactions around the question more man-ageable, and the classroom response system technology provides a way for all students to participate, even selecting their choice before hearing what others have to say. And all students get feedback on their efforts, whether that's hearing a "good reasoning" from Law after they contribute to the class discussion or simply finding out whether their treatment choice was one of the better ones. A good multiple-choice question used with a classroom response system can create effective all-skate opportunities for practice and feedback, even in very large classes.

Classroom response systems aren't the only tools useful for cre-ating all-skate environments, of course. Google Docs, for instance, can provide collaborative spaces for student practice during class, as we'll see in chapter 5, and Twitter can provide more opportunities for student contributions than class time might otherwise permit. Nontechnological approaches can help, too, including jigsaws and structured reading groups.[22] The key is to look for tools and strategies that invite all students to participate, not just the fastest or boldest students. That said, classroom response systems are flexible technol-ogies for supporting in-class learning activities. That's why I'm using them as examples in the first few chapters of this book, which focus on the classroom context. I think all instructors should be familiar with the options classroom response systems provide for creating times for telling, practice and feedback, and, as we'll see in the next chapter, making student learning visible.

Practical Advice

Given all the different cognitive skills students might need to practice, there are many, many ways to use technology to build opportunities for practice and feedback. The examples in this chapter just scratch the surface, and I always encourage instructors to think creatively about ways to build practice into their class sessions. But the examples here also point to some general advice that's often relevant when leveraging technology for skill-building.

1.   Consider the skills your students need to practice, and build class activities around those skills. For instance, Lendol Calder writes that historians need to be able to question, to connect, to source, to make inferences, to consider alternative perspectives, and to recognize the limits of one's knowledge. He has his students practice one or more of these skills in each class session of his history survey course.[23] You might find it helpful to consider a final paper or project in your course and unpack the skills your students will need to succeed in that project, then plan opportunities for students to practice those skills.

2.   If you're already giving students homework that asks them to practice working with the concepts and techniques they encounter in class, consider moving that homework into the class session itself. As noted above, this move lies at the heart of the flipped classroom—giving students the chance to practice learning during class, when their peers and their instructor are around to help. Richard Flagan made that move when he asked his students to program together during class, and Kathryn Tomasek did, too, when she had her students practice text encoding together as a class.

3. To organize in-class practice, start with a simple structure like the classic think-pair-share. First, have students work on a problem individually for a minute or two (think). Then have them get together in small groups to discuss their work (pair). Finally, ask students to report out to the whole class (share). There are lots of ways to modify this structure—have students free-write during the think phase, varying the group size during the pair phase, using a classroom response system for sharing, and so on—and it tends to work well no matter how the seating is arranged in a particular classroom.

4. Crunched for time for in-class practice and feedback? Consider shifting some introductory material to pre-class activities. A well-chosen reading or a short explanatory video can go a long way to getting students ready for in-class activities, especially if there's some form of accountability involved in the pre-class work, like an online quiz or a required blog posting. But be mindful that for some topics, an experiential first encounter is more productive than an explanatory one, as we saw in chapter 1.

5. Be sure to build feedback mechanisms into your in-class activities. Aggregate feedback can work well: "It looks like a lot of you chose option B. Here's what's problematic about that option . . ." Individual feedback is often more useful, but hard to do in an all-skate way. Group work can help, since students can provide feedback to each other and group time provides you opportunities to circulate among students and interact.

6. Bear in mind that students aren't always expecting class time to be used for practice and feedback. Asking students to work in groups, to solve problems, to use technology in on-topic ways during class can sometimes surprise students. Be sure to communicate clearly to students the value of using class time for practice and feedback. Start from the beginning, building active learning exercises into the first day of class to set expectations.

7. When it comes to using technology for practice and feedback, you have a range of options. Are you teaching a course in the

major, preparing students for future work in your discipline? Then it might be worth the time and effort to teach them to use discipline-specific tools, like MATLAB or TEI. But in an introductory course, more general technologies, like a classroom response system or a course blog, might be more practical. And tell your students why you're using a particular tool for a particular activity, as Cornelia Lang does in her active learning classrooms.

8.   We often have some trepidation about asking students to get out their phones or laptops during class. However, many instructors find that when they give their students something productive to do with their mobile devices (beyond just taking notes), students don't use them (as much) in off-topic ways. That said, don't be afraid to ask your students to put their devices away or to close their laptop lids after the activity is concluded.

9.   Bear in mind, however, that not every student will have a mobile device for use during class. Group work, again, can help with this, since you often only need one device per group. But if access is an issue in your classroom, talk to colleagues at the library or in IT about loaner devices for your students. You might also find that the financial aid office has options for students taking classes where technology is required. And consider technologies that allow a range of response methods, from Web to apps to text messaging, so a broader set of devices can be used.

10. One more piece of advice: use technology to make student learning visible so that you can be more responsive to your students' learning needs. That bit of advice is important enough—and complex enough—that it's the focus of the entire next chapter.

There's an adage in math education that you can't learn mathematics by watching mathematics; you have to do mathematics. That's true in all our disciplines, and providing students ways to do your discipline is a sensible way to leverage educational technology.

CHAPTER 3

Thin Slices of Learning

A COUPLE of years ago, my teenage daughter decided to make a short film. She got an idea for a film based on the word *sonder*, the realization that everyone else has as rich and complex a life as you do. She drafted a script, corralled some friends from her drama class, borrowed some equipment, and spent winter break shooting and editing her film. The result was indeed a short film, just under two minutes, but she submitted it to a film festival in California that had a student division, where it got accepted and screened. We flew out to San Luis Obispo to see her film on the big screen, and we were surprised and thrilled when she won the "Best Drama" award for the student division.[1] I couldn't have been a prouder dad at that moment.

Over the course of multiple days of shooting that winter break, my daughter filmed three hours of footage—three hours for what resulted in a two-minute film. That's a shooting ratio of 90 to 1, that is, 90 minutes of raw footage for 1 minute of running time. That ratio isn't unusual for this medium. One film editor estimated that the shooting ratio for the 2015 feature film *The Martian* was 104 to 1, with 250 hours of footage for a 144-minute film.[2] The 2014 film *Gone Girl* had a shooting ratio of 149 to 1, and *Mad Max: Fury Road* (2015) was even more extreme, with a ratio of 240 to 1. By way of contrast, the 2004 independent (and seriously head scratching) time travel film *Primer* is reported to have had a shooting ratio of 1.04 to 1, which means almost every scene was shot in a single take. That's nuts.

Considering a major motion picture like *The Martian* or a no-budget independent short film like my daughter's *Sonder*, there's a lot that gets left out of the final cut of a film—multiple takes of the same shot, different angles of the same scene, entire scenes or plotlines, whole characters. An editor has to weigh each piece of footage and decide what role it might play in the final product, then make hard decisions about what to include and what to cut. A viewer wouldn't know this from looking at the finished film, of course, if the editor has done a good job. But there are hundreds or thousands of little decisions an editor has to make along the way to the film that makes it to screen, and those decisions require analysis, evaluation, and expertise.

Years ago, I heard Georgetown University's Randall Bass speak to this at a conference on the scholarship of teaching and learning. In his keynote, he described a digital storytelling project he assigned one of his American studies courses. He noted that it was challenging to evaluate the students' final short videos by just viewing the videos. "There was so much learning," Bass said, "that was left on the cutting room floor." Later, he captured this idea for a piece he wrote on the future of higher education.[3] Arguing for a shift in the focus of course design from content to practice, Bass wrote, "Three or four decades of research has taught us that a lot of meaningful activity—struggling, processing, sense-making—is going on in the intermediate space between novice and expert."

Just as much of the work of a film editor isn't visible in a finished film, much of the learning that our students experience isn't captured in a final paper or project. The results of an editor's choices can be seen on screen, and the results of our students' learning shows up in the assignments they turn in. But if we really wanted to understand a film editor's decision-making process, we would need to see them in action, as they cut and splice and edit. And if we really want to understand and respond to our students' learning—the "struggling, processing, sense-making" that Bass mentions—we have to find ways to make our students' learning visible as they go about their work.

> **PRINCIPLE 3.** *The more we understand about what and how our students are learning, the more responsive we can be to their learning needs.*

This is the work of formative assessment, the assessment of learning that happens along the way to inform instruction and provide students useful feedback. Contrast this with summative assessment, the thumbs-up-thumbs-down evaluation of student work that comes at the end of a learning process. That's important, but it comes too late to shape and inform instruction. Formative assessment provides us insights into our students' learning—what and how they are learning, what misconceptions or misperceptions they struggle with—as they are learning, allowing us to be more responsive to their learning needs.

Technology can be great for formative assessment. And it can be particularly effective in making visible what Bass calls "thin slices" of student learning, the little bits of learning that are easy to miss if we're not attentive.[4] When we make those thin slices visible, we meet our students in that "intermediate space between novice and expert," allowing us to better understand our students and help them as they build and develop their expertise. The examples that follow feature instructors using technology in just this way.

Social Bookmarking and Credible Sources

The cryptography seminar I teach is the best course. Sorry, every other course, but it's true. It's a first-year writing seminar on codes and ciphers and privacy and surveillance. We spend a week on Alan Turing and the Enigma machine and the military cryptography of World War II. We spend another week on Edward Snowden and the NSA and the role of encryption in our digital lives. I usually organize some kind of cryptography-themed scavenger hunt or escape room; there are weekly problem sets and a math exam, multiple writing assignments, occasionally a student-produced podcast; and, oh yeah, I teach a novel. (More on that novel and how I teach it in chapter 4.) And, best of all, there are only fifteen students in the course and most of them want to be there, since they picked my crypto course out of a slate of first-year writing seminars offered across the college. Some years, the students in the course create a text messaging group that lasts long after the semester is over, as students continue to share stories about cryptography in the news.

As great as it is to teach a course that has such enthusiastic students, they're still students, and all of them struggle with one part of the course or another. It's a writing seminar, and I always include a traditional research paper, where students have to make an argument using evidence from credible sources. The course features a number of nontraditional assignments (again, see later chapters), but since one of the goals of the first-year writing seminar is to prepare students for work in future courses, I feel it's important to give students a traditional research paper. Plus, I find that the argumentative essay is a useful way to have students really dig into the privacy versus security debate that we explore during Edward Snowden week and throughout the course. It's a hard assignment for my students, since they have to do enough research to form an interesting thesis, then support that thesis with a variety of arguments, all backed up by evidence.

I'm often surprised by the elements of this final paper assignment that challenge my students. A few years ago, I stumbled upon a method for surfacing some of these surprises well before the assignment was handed out. As part of an online participation grade, I asked my students to engage in what's known as *social bookmarking*.[5] Your favorite Web browser certainly has some kind of bookmarking feature, where you can save links to websites for later reference. The downside of browser bookmarks is that they're only available while using that browser on that computer. Social bookmarking tools, on the other hand, allow one to save a link to the cloud, where it can be accessed by any browser on any computer with the right login. Moreover, these tools allow one to make a bookmark public so that others can view it, and some social bookmarking platforms have group functions that enable a number of users to create shared collections of bookmarks.

That's how I use social bookmarking in my cryptography course. I create a group for my students on the social bookmarking site Diigo, and I ask my students to contribute links to useful resources regularly throughout the course.[6] The first time I did this, I asked my students to bookmark ten useful or interesting websites throughout the course and to tag each bookmark with three or more keywords. The result was a collection of more than 150 links relevant to the course, collected by my students and tagged for easy searching. Every week or two, I selected a few of the most interesting bookmarks and projected them on the big screen during class for ten minutes of discussion. The upside of this assignment was a rich collection of resources relevant to the course, exploring aspects of cryptography that my individual students found compelling. The downside was that half of my students waited until the final week of the course to contribute their bookmarks, which wasn't ideal.

Learning from this experiment, the next time I taught the course, I structured the social bookmarking assignment a little differently. Instead of giving students free rein to find and bookmark resources on their own time, I gave the students specific bookmarking assignments every other week during the semester. For example, early in the course I asked my students to bookmark examples of cryptography in the news. During our World War II unit, I asked students to find and bookmark resources on military cryptography. I also asked students to find real-life examples of some of the surveillance and privacy practices mentioned in the novel we read together. This more structured approach kept students contributing to the class bookmark collection regularly, and it helped ensure that I could make good use of the resources they found and shared.

Here's the "thin slices" angle: The bookmark assignments also reveal to me some gaps my students have in their preparation for the evidence-based writing assignments I give them later in the semester. One year, a few weeks into the course, I asked students to "bookmark a credible source of news or information about cryptography." I suggested they bookmark a journal that focused on the history of cryptography, the blog of a scholar who researches online privacy issues, or the Twitter feed of a journalist who covers cybersecurity. I used the next class session as an opportunity to talk with the students about sources and what makes a source credible, using the sources they had found for the bookmarking assignment.

We talked about how a cybersecurity firm might have useful expertise on, say, identity theft or virtual private networks but might also have commercial interests that could bias its recommendations. We talked about standards of journalism that lead to some news outlets' being more credible than some guy with a blog. And after noting that none of the students had identified individual journalists who covered privacy issues, I pointed to a few journalist Twitter accounts I know to be reliable sources of current information, and I shared with the students how I follow their work to stay up-to-date on the news. This last item turned into its own bookmarking assignment in a subsequent offering of the course, in which I asked students specifically to identify journalists I should add to a list I maintain of Twitter accounts relevant to the course. That list is now more useful thanks to my students' contributions.

Finding a variety of credible sources for a given topic is a critical skill for students working on research papers in an academic context. If I wait to help my students develop this skill the week before their papers are due, it's too late. This social bookmarking assignment is one small way I can assess my students' skills in this area well before a major assignment, identify where they have gaps, and provide them feedback and direction. That is, the contributions my students make to our class Diigo group make visible this little piece of their learning in a way that lets me respond and be helpful.

Tweets from the Field

This next example is my favorite use of Twitter in teaching. Margaret Rubega is a biologist at the University of Connecticut and also Connecticut's state ornithologist. Her research and public scholarship are all about birds, and she teaches an ornithology course at UConn. It's a large class, usually with a hundred or so students from a wide variety of academic backgrounds. Many of them come to the course thinking that birds are pretty cool but that all the interesting birds are far away, in exotic places like the Amazon or China. They get this impression from the nature documentaries they've seen, but Rubega wants her students to "appreciate that the amazing, incredible things we talk about in lecture, the way that biology plays out in birds, is something that they can literally walk out of the building and see happening on the sidewalk right on campus."[7]

To help her students see that the birds in Connecticut are fascinating, too, Rubega asks her students to take to Twitter and tweet about the birds they see as they go about their daily lives. Once a week, students post their observations, including information about what they see, where they are, and the connections they find from their observation to course content. For instance, here are a few student tweets from the spring 2015 ornithology course:

- "Laying by mirror lake just spotted a crow/sparrow dive bombing a hawk, looks like someone's protecting their territory! #birdclass" —@MDaudBirds (Mary Daudish)
- "went golfing today and heard 5 distinct calls from various bird species. The design of the fairways seems to divide territories #birdclass" —@Zach_UConn (Zachary Skelton)
- "So many songbirds in the top of a bare tree near from horsebarn, the branch was bowed; best acoustics or safety in numbers perhaps #birdclass" —@MALinsenbigler (Megan Linsenbigler)

Pictures aren't required, but some of Rubega's students are handy with a camera, as seen in figures 4 and 5. The tweet in figure 4 reads, "This WTSP [white-throated sparrow] at the HEEP site this morning must be eating tons of carotenoids to produce such vibrant lores! #birdclass," and the one in figure 5 says, "If it wasn't for broken wing display, I wouldn't have noticed this camouflaged Killdeer nest on the levee! #birdclass." Both tweets include photos taken by the students of their observations.

All of these tweets include the hashtag #birdclass. Rubega asks her students to include this hashtag to make their tweets easier to find on Twitter. Clicking on the hashtag brings up all tweets that use the hashtag, and anyone can visit search.twitter.com and search for the hashtag to see the latest tweets from Rubega's students. (Go

Figure 4. Screenshot of #birdclass tweet by student Kali Block.

ahead and try. I'll wait here.) Hashtags serve a variety of purposes on Twitter, from creative self-expression to something like keywords you see in a library catalog entry. In this case, the hashtag creates a kind of virtual community for the students in Rubega's course, as well as others (like me) who follow the course from afar. Students are able to see each other do their homework, and Rubega finds this creates a kind of positive peer pressure for students to look for birds as they travel between home and campus and work.

Twitter is an ideal medium for this assignment. The 140-character

Figure 5. Screenshot of #birdclass tweet by student Victoria Heyse.

(now 280-character) limit forces concision but is just enough space to meet the assignment requirements—observation, location, and course connection. (Rubega grades the assignment lightly, on a three-point scale, depending on how many of the three requirements are included in the tweets.) Students can post tweets from their phones, right from the field. If for some reason students can't tweet from their phones in the moment, they can always write down their observations and post their work from twitter.com when they're back at a computer. And, as seen above, Twitter handles multimedia well, including photos and videos. There's a subtlety here, too, as the assignment turns the phone that most students carry with them everywhere into a field observation device. The phone's very presence helps to remind students to look for birds along their way.

Thus the assignment helps the students practice what's called *transfer*. We want our students to take what they're learning in our classrooms and apply it to new problems and situations when they leave us. This kind of applied learning is really hard, and students need lots of practice with it.[8] Rubega's #birdclass assignment provides transfer practice on a regular basis, asking students to take what they're learning in lecture and apply it to the real-world lab they experience every day. And by asking her students to engage in this kind of transfer practice on Twitter, Rubega gets a little window into their learning, into the sense they're making of the course material. She can respond directly to student tweets, praising an on-target insight or great photo or providing some gentle feedback when a student makes an incorrect conclusion. Rubega can also share particularly interesting tweets with the whole class during class meetings, helping all students learn from the observations of a single student. (We'll return to this aspect of the assignment in chapter 6.)

Transfer is hard, but by giving her students opportunities to practice transfer and making that practice visible to her and to fellow students, Rubega can find out how well her students are engaging in this work and provide useful feedback along the way. I've seen Twitter used in similar ways in very different courses: for instance, teacher education courses in which preservice teachers tweet their observations about learning dynamics in the classrooms they observe, or civil engineering courses in which students tweet observations of structural mechanics they see in the built environment around them. Twitter isn't essential to these activities—posts to a course management system discussion board would work, too—but Twitter makes these assignments easy and interactive and fun. Getting a response or retweet from their instructor or a fellow student or even a total stranger can provide a little reward for a student who makes an interesting observation.

Beyond the activity's "thin slices" potential, there's a strong motivational component, too, as Rubega has found. She reports that students initially uninterested in birds, taking the course just to fulfill a requirement, sometimes end up quite passionate about the topic, correcting total strangers on Twitter who mix up their swallows and swifts! One semester Rubega was traveling in Belize over spring break. She hadn't told her students where she was going, and, on a lark, she tweeted her bird list (the list of birds she had spotted that day) and challenged her students to figure out where she was. Even though it was spring break, three of her students responded, triangulating her location by looking up the geographic distributions of the birds she named. One student said to her later, "I learned more about geography in that tweet exchange than I did in all of high school!"

Livetweeting the Reading

Twitter seems particularly well suited to making visible thin slices of student learning. Back in 2009, I heard about the "Twitter experiment" conducted by history professor Monica Rankin at the University of Texas at Dallas.[9] That spring, she added a Twitter layer to the Friday class sessions in her US history survey course. Students discussed a set of prompts in small groups and were encouraged to share their insights and questions via Twitter using a class hashtag. Rankin projected the class tweets on the big screen and occasionally paused the small group discussion to talk about particular tweets with the entire class. Twitter functioned as a backchannel, supplementing the "front channel" of class discussion by allowing ideas and concerns to cross over from small group to small group.[10]

Twitter as backchannel can add depth to a class discussion and provide useful insights into how students are thinking about course materials, particularly students who are less vocal in face-to-face conversations. However, talking with instructors who have experimented with this use of Twitter, I have found that many instructors find the backchannel too hard to keep up with, especially when they have front-of-the-room responsibilities, lecturing or leading whole-class discussion. Adding a backchannel to small group discussion, as professor Rankin did, or creating targeted "backchannel breaks" during class, when students are given two or three minutes to engage in backchannel conversations, is more manageable than anything-goes backchannel use, but more structured Twitter assignments, like the #birdclass assignment, seem to have more utility for most instructors.

Mark Sample, now a digital studies professor at Davidson College, used one such structured Twitter assignment for a 2011 science fiction course he taught at George Mason University. At one point in the course, the week's "reading" was actually a viewing of the Ridley Scott film *Blade Runner*. Sample wasn't screening the film during class, so he asked his students to watch the film on their own at some point during the week before the class discussion of the film. To "create a collective experience out of these disparate viewings," Sample asked his students to livetweet the film as they watched it.[11] And they did. Collectively, they posted hundreds of tweets over the week. A few examples:

- "He's trying to prove that he's not a replicant by trying to fall in love, develop emotions. Even tho he knows he is. #ENGH451" —@poor_atlas (Forrest)
- "i really love this detective/private eye style narration, and it's interesting how the setting reminds me of the one in neuromancer #engh451" —@superdude85 (Brian Ko)
- "any time somebody hunts you in their underwear you know they mean business #ENGH451" —@Wangle4 (Will)

Some tweets were funny, some were insightful, and some, like that second tweet, drew connections between *Blade Runner* and other texts from the course. Before the class discussion, Sample collected and organized the student tweets using a now-defunct tool called Storify. He sorted the tweets by theme (intertexts and allusions, visual design, what it means to be human, and so on), then used those themes to structure the class discussion of the film.

It's common practice to have students read a text or watch a film and write a brief response paper before class. That's a useful practice, since it encourages students to reflect on the week's text and draw connections to other texts or conversations. What I like about Sample's livetweeting assignment, however, is that it captures in-the-moment observations that might not make it into a student's response paper. These observations provide a window into a learning space that we don't often get to see, especially when that space lands outside of class time. And Sample was able to look through that window and prepare differently for class discussion because of what he learned about his students' experience of the film. How often do we have this level of granularity in the perspectives and ideas our students bring to a class discussion?

Simply asking students to livetweet the reading prompts them to be more attentive and critical readers. It signals to students that their initial impressions as they encounter a text are important and can lead to deeper discussions down the road. There's also a social benefit to this kind of assignment, as students see each other's tweets during the week leading up to the class discussion and are encouraged to "do the reading" themselves in time for class. Moreover, the collected tweets, organized by theme, provide a set of notes on the text that students can reference later in the course as they encounter other texts or work on assignments.

That same semester, Sample also asked his students to livetweet their experiences playing the video game *Portal*, and I can imagine other livetweeting opportunities in other courses. One might ask students to tweet questions that occur to them as they read their textbooks before class, connections they make while doing research for a major assignment, highlights from group meetings for large projects, or observations made during a class field trip or evening event.[12] One important component of Sample's assignments is the flow from out-of-class individual work to in-class conversations. If there's not an in-class follow-up to the out-of-class tweeting, then the activity can feel like busywork to students. But when students realize that their preparations for class time can inform and shape what happens during class, they often take the entire sequence of learning activities more seriously.

This is also a good time to say a word about student privacy. When we ask students to make their learning visible through Twitter or some other technology, some students might be uncomfortable doing so, particularly in a way that identifies them. In fact, that's one element of FERPA, the Family Educational Rights and Privacy Act, the law that governs student privacy in the United States. Among other things, FERPA means that the fact that student X is enrolled in course Y is information that instructors can't require students to disclose. Students should get the choice to disclose that information or not. This means that asking students to use their real name on social media for a class assignment can be problematic. Two advantages of using Twitter are that the service doesn't require real names and that it allows users to create multiple accounts. If a student doesn't want their name associated in public with their course work, they can create a new Twitter account, one that doesn't include their name, just for that purpose.

Students might also be uncomfortable with the risk that comes along with learning in public. In a classroom, students can usually opt out of conversations or be selective about what they share. It's appropriate to extend that ability to students participating in online spaces. Students in Mark Sample's science fiction course, for instance, weren't required to livetweet all their observations of *Blade Runner*. They could choose which ones to share. More fundamentally, however, if the purpose of a structured Twitter assignment is to make visible thin slices of student learning, that is, if it's meant to be formative assessment, keeping the stakes low can help students feel comfortable participating, as can telling students that it's okay to be wrong or take a risk at this stage of the learning process. A half-formed thought about *Blade Runner* while you're watching it might turn into a well-developed argument in a paper later in the semester, which is why creating spaces for these initial impressions can be really valuable.

Making Learning Audible

Sometimes, making student learning visible isn't as helpful as making student learning audible. Ashley Hasty teaches merchandising at Indiana University at Bloomington. A few years ago in her visual merchandising class, she added a service-learning assignment in which students work in small groups to design and construct window displays for local nonprofit organizations. Not all nonprofits have window displays, but some do, and they often can't afford the services of a professional merchandiser. By asking her students to build displays for these local nonprofits, she gives her students the chance to apply what they're learning about visual merchandising with an actual client and work within the constraints that brings, and she provides a potentially useful service for nonprofits in and around Bloomington.

Hasty asked students to submit photos of their finished window displays, and she graded their work according to the design tools and rules she taught them earlier in the course—line, color, shape, texture, balance, sequence, surprise, tension, and more. She quickly ran into two problems. One was that students weren't always able to implement the tools and rules as she taught them, given the constraints placed on their work by their clients. That is, students sometimes had to choose between good design and satisfying the client, and they tended to choose the client. That choice, as intentional as it was for her students, wasn't visible in their final work, so their grades suffered, since Hasty's evaluation was based on how she saw her students apply theory to practice. The other problem was that, as Hasty told me, "Some students had really great displays, but they had no idea why they were good. They couldn't articulate why a display looks better one way, and not the other." Some of her best designers lacked the vocabulary to describe the choices they were making.

In an effort to solve these problems, Hasty started using a tool called VoiceThread with the assignment. Students could use VoiceThread to upload a photo of their window display, then add audio annotations to particular locations within the photo. Hasty asked her students to use the tool to explain the choices they made during their design process. For instance, a student might circle one corner of their display (using VoiceThread's pen tool) and add an audio note explaining why they used particular colors or materials in that part of the window display. Or they might point to a lighting fixture they incorporated in their display, noting through audio that their client required them to use that fixture. This solved the problem about the occasional mismatch between design principles and client constraints, and it gave students the opportunity to put words to their design choices. VoiceThread allowed Hasty to hear the student learning that was, to quote Randy Bass again, "left on the cutting room floor."

In fact, Hasty discovered so much about her students' learning through the audio annotations they left in VoiceThread that she stopped grading the window displays themselves and instead graded the students' reflections on the displays. The VoiceThread annotations allowed Hasty to evaluate her students' intentionality and how they worked with limitations. As the semester went on, she gave students increasingly complex questions to respond to in their annotations, and they really took to it, preparing remarks before hitting Record and sometimes talking about their design choices for twenty or thirty minutes. Hasty had to institute a ten-minute recording limit just to make her grading manageable!

Moreover, the annotations allowed her to provide individual grades on group projects. Each group created a single window display and uploaded photos of the display to VoiceThread, but individual group members added their own layers of audio commentary. Since Hasty had moved to evaluating a student's reflection on the work, not the collective work itself, she could provide differential grades to group members. This had the added benefit of revealing connections between group dynamics and finished work. For instance, she could hear how two group members with different ideas about some aspect of their display reached a compromise choice and how that choice could be seen in the final display.

Once Hasty realized she could use VoiceThread audio annotations as formative assessment, she found other ways to use the tool in her course. For instance, she directed her students to an archive of historical window displays dating back to the 1930s and asked students to analyze them using the design principles they were learning in the course, allowing her to assess how well her students were understanding and applying those principles. One semester, the service-learning projects didn't work out, so she asked students to upload photos of existing (modern) window displays they didn't create. Multiple students would then analyze the same display, resulting in a healthy back-and-forth as they agreed and disagreed with each other's analyses.

Beyond the formative assessment capabilities, VoiceThread provided Hasty's students a way to reflect on their learning that was more authentic to their future careers in visual merchandising. "You would never," said Hasty, "hand a paper to someone and say, this is why I did my visual display this way." But you might have a supervisor come over and explain to her verbally the choices you made as you designed your display. In this way, Hasty helped her students not only develop expertise but articulate that expertise in disciplinary authentic ways. And, Hasty added, listening to students talk about their creative work was way more fun than reading another paper.

Thin Slices of Marker Board

"Whiteboards are almost as fast as their thinking."

Tracy Ruscetti teaches biology at Santa Clara University, and she makes use of an analog technology that's been around for a while to make student learning visible. In her upper-level microbiology course, she assigns half-a-dozen group assessments each semester. Students complete these assessments in teams of six, and the assessments typically have a jigsaw structure: each student in the group studies a different aspect of a topic before class and the in-class activity requires the group to leverage their collective expertise to solve a problem. This takes collaboration, and Ruscetti has found that the

Figure 6. Small whiteboards in Tracy Ruscetti's biology class. Photo by Derek Bruff.

best collaboration tool is often an old-fashioned dry-erase board, also known as a whiteboard. Each group is given their own small whiteboard, maybe eighteen inches by twenty-four inches, on which to brainstorm, revise, and document their group solution (fig. 6). Her students find the whiteboards easy to draw on, easy to erase, and easy to edit. This fluidity of use helps them capture their thinking as it evolves, almost in real time.

For example, in one group assessment, students are asked to construct a decision tree (like a flow chart) they would follow when using laboratory tests to identify unknown microorganisms. The laboratory tests are interdependent, and students need to decide which tests to perform and in what order. For example, if a Gram stain test is positive, then students may choose to perform a spore stain next, but if the result is Gram-negative, then a different test might be more appropriate. There are many different possible decision trees, and students use the whiteboards to "sample" the available solution space, with the goal of constructing a tree that uses the fewest number of tests in the shortest amount of time. Once a group of students has settled on the most efficient decision tree, they photograph the final product with their phones and submit that photo for assessment. Later in lab, students perform their own bacteria identification by using a decision tree they develop based on the same thought processes they practiced collaboratively in class.

Ruscetti has tried having students use digital collaboration tools, like Google Draw, for this type of group assignment. However, she finds that these tools aren't responsive enough, aren't "almost as fast as their thinking." Also, students aren't willing to erase their work using digital tools, and they need to erase and start over when tackling hard problems like the ones in these team activities. "There's an impermanence to the whiteboards," Ruscetti told me, "that the students aren't committing to a particular idea." They can play with it, see where it goes, and keep it only if it's useful. "If they make a mistake, that's okay, it's not permanent." The whiteboard work feels like a first draft, which it needs to be as the students learn from and with each other.

Small, portable whiteboards (sometimes called "huddle boards") are also useful because they're right there, says Peter Newbury, director of the Centre for Teaching and Learning at the University of British Columbia's Okanagan campus. With a whiteboard hanging on the end of every group table, the collaborative space whiteboards create is immediately available to students. There's no need to move to a workspace on the wall or a laptop and thus no need to interrupt student engagement with problem solving. Newbury has seen instructors use small, portable whiteboards in a variety of courses, and he uses them in his own professional development workshops for faculty and other instructors. For instance, he might have workshop participants quickly draft learning objectives for their courses on their whiteboards, then swap whiteboards with a partner to edit and revise. Or, if the whiteboards are magnetic, Newbury will have participants attach papers or cards with magnetic backing to the boards, then annotate their groupings and arrangements using markers, not unlike how Ashley Hasty uses VoiceThread to have students verbally annotate their photos.

Like Ruscetti, Newbury also finds that whiteboards encourage better brainstorming. Give students a big sheet of paper and a marker they can use to show their work to the class, and they will wait to write down their "perfect" final answer. That's a reporting tool, not a thinking tool. On the other hand, give students a small whiteboard and a little encouragement that it's okay to make mistakes, and they will jump in and start thinking with their pens. "The whiteboard," Newbury told me, "reveals the development of the students' answers, and it reveals incomplete thinking, misconceptions, the places where people make errors. It's the perfect place to try, fail, get feedback, and try again."

And whiteboards used in this way make student learning visible in the moment to instructors as they circulate among their students. "Deciding whether or not to intervene," Newbury said, "that's the teaching moment. Do you let them go or do you interrupt?" If students are just talking in groups as they work collaboratively on a problem, an instructor can't always tell what they're saying and thus decide whether to intervene. The instructor can sit with a group of students and listen for a while, but their presence changes the social learning dynamic. If students are documenting their thinking on a whiteboard, however, an instructor can eavesdrop at a distance, spotting groups from across the room that need a little extra help or feedback. And if each student in a group is using a different marker color, an instructor can provide even more directed help, asking about a calculation mistake made in green or praising a good idea written in blue, for instance.

Making student learning visible to instructors is useful, as is making learning visible to other students. For instance, Ruscetti asks her students to draw concept maps for particular topics, simple diagrams of concepts and their relationships. (See chapter 4 on knowledge organizations for more on this visual tool.) Then she asks her students to trade whiteboards and add what's missing to their partner's concept map in a different marker color. This activity makes learning by both students visible and thus helps students learn from each other. Ruscetti also uses a practice called a *gallery walk*. Students all diagram the same structure or process on their individual whiteboards, then prop up those whiteboards on the floor around the room. Students then walk around the room, considering the different visual heuristics their peers used in their diagrams, sometimes voting on the best visual heuristic they see. They learn as they see their peers illustrate their learning.

Small, portable whiteboards aren't fancy, and they don't have to be expensive. You can find instructions online for building your own from cheap materials available at your local hardware store. Sometimes I hear it said that active learning instruction requires high-tech classrooms, like Cornelia Lang's TILE classroom described in the last chapter. However, there's some evidence that the low-tech elements of an active learning classroom, the tables and whiteboards, are the most important elements.[13] As Peter Newbury says, "High tech is neither necessary nor sufficient for active learning." To engage students in collaborative learning and to make that learning visible as it develops, sometimes all it takes is a simple whiteboard and a well-structured group activity.

Agile Teaching

Small, portable whiteboards are powerful because they help make student learning visible during class, when the instructor is present and available to respond to student learning needs. When we practice formative assessment during class and respond in the moment to what we discover about our students' particular learning needs, we engage what I like to call *agile teaching*. Contrast this with what Ian Beatty and colleagues call *ballistic teaching*. That's when you launch a lesson plan at the start of the hour and nothing can interfere with its trajectory until it's done.[14] A traditional college lecture often functions that way, especially when it's planned down to the minute. Agile teaching, on the other hand, involves finding out what students are learning, what misconceptions and difficulties they have, and what perspectives and experiences they bring to the table, then meeting that particular group of students where they are and helping them go deeper with the material.

In the last chapter, I described ways classroom response systems can create all-skate environments in the classroom. These systems, whether they use dedicated clicker devices or make use of students' own mobile devices, are also great at facilitating agile teaching. Consider a clicker question used by Elizabeth Cullingford in her large-enrollment literature class at the University of Texas–Austin. After having her students read Shakespeare's *Hamlet*, she asked her students the following question:

Hamlet's lines following the death of Ophelia suggest that:

A. Hamlet really loved Ophelia and is so distraught to learn of her death that he proposes to eat a crocodile.
B. Hamlet thinks that Laertes's grief is mere posturing and mocks it by exaggeration.
C. Hamlet cares little for Ophelia but is eager to enter into a rhetorical chest-thumping competition with her brother.

As I described in my previous book, Cullingford asked her students to respond to this question using clickers, then projected the distribution of responses on the big screen at the front of the room.[15] Starting with the more popular answer choices, she asked for student volunteers to defend their answers to the class. For the least popular response, she played devil's advocate, arguing for that choice using textual evidence in the play to support her argument. She wanted to model for her students how to make a textual argument, and she wanted her students to realize that, in fact, all three choices are defensible given what we know about the character of Hamlet in the play. The clicker question helped her identify which of the three responses made the least sense to her students in terms of how they might argue for it using the text, then she spent class time unpacking that response to help students understand how they could defend it. That's agile teaching, and it's particularly impressive in Cullingford's case, since this was done in a class with two hundred to three hundred students!

Or consider the following classroom response system activity I regularly use in my first-year writing course. Before the first paper assignment is due, I ask for a student volunteer to share their draft paper with the entire class. I distribute copies of the draft paper along with the rubric I will use to grade the students' papers. The rubric usually consists of eight or nine categories ranging from "clarity of thesis" to "relevance of argument" to "mechanics." Within each category, the rubric includes descriptors for four levels of quality: poor, acceptable, good, excellent. For instance, here are the descriptors for the category "complexity of argument":

1. Poor—The student fails to consider positions other than the one for which s/he argues in the paper.
2. Acceptable—The student considers alternate positions or potential objections to his/her arguments but offers no significant response to those other positions.
3. Good—The student considers alternate positions or potential objections and offers some responses to those positions.

4. Excellent—The student considers several potential objections to his/her arguments and offers appropriate and perhaps compelling counter-arguments.

I ask all students, including the volunteer who shared their draft, to read the draft paper and evaluate it using the rubric, rating the paper as poor, acceptable, good, or excellent in each of the categories specified by the rubric. After they have done so, I ask students to submit their ratings in each category using the classroom response system. Taking one category at a time, we review the distributions of student ratings on the projector screen.

Sometimes, there's a lot of consensus. For instance, it might be that most students rated the paper as excellent in "clarity of thesis" because of an explicitly stated thesis statement, while most students rated the paper as only acceptable in "clarity of argument" because of a few very unclear paragraphs. For other categories, however, there's less consensus among the students. For example, I usually ask my students to make a personal connection to the topic of their first paper, and they often find this challenging. (One reason: some students are told by their high school English teachers never to use first-person pronouns in academic writing.) When evaluating the draft paper in the "personal connection" category, students are often all over the map, some rating it poor, others excellent. And there's often similar disagreement over ratings in "complexity of argument," since that's a hard aspect of writing for first-year students to grasp, and also "mechanics," since some student set the bar really high for grammar ("Never start a sentence with a conjunction!") but others don't.

When we reach one of these categories where there isn't student consensus, I ask students to justify their ratings by identifying particular places in the draft paper that showed or lacked quality. The discussion invariably ends with one student asking me how I would evaluate the draft paper in the given category. This gives me a chance to clarify my expectations for my students' writing, using a process that identifies specific areas where there's a mismatch between my expectations and my students' expectations. And since we engage in this process a few days before their final papers are due, students have the chance to take what they've learned about my expectations for their writing and apply it to their work on the assignment.

Note that the technology is critical in this example. Students will rarely critique a peer publicly, but if everyone rates the draft paper as excellent in every category, just to be nice to the author, this activity goes nowhere. Allowing students to evaluate their peer's work anonymously, using the classroom response system, makes this activity work. Similarly, in Elizabeth Cullingford's class, asking students to respond to the question about Hamlet with a show of hands might not elicit honest student responses, given that students are often wary of looking incorrect in front of their peers. The anonymity provided by a classroom response system is one reason such systems are useful tools for making student learning—especially thin slices of student learning—visible during class. And the ability of these systems to quickly display a distribution of student responses gives instructors actionable information to practice agile teaching and to respond to the particular learning needs their students have.

Practical Advice

There are as many different ways to use technology to make student learning visible as there are lessons that students might learn. That said, instructors wanting a peek inside their students' heads through formative assessment should consider the following choices and suggestions.

1. Be clear on what you want your students to learn, then find ways to make that learning visible. That is, align your formative assessment efforts with your learning objectives. This kind of alignment is critical to the design of effective learning experiences.[16] Margaret Rubega wanted her students to recognize bird behavior and ecology in the world outside their window, and her #birdclass Twitter assignment asked students to do exactly that.

2. Look for aspects of final assignments and projects where students struggle and build formative assessment activities around those problem areas. That way you can identify and assist with trouble spots well before those issues trip students up on big assignments. I saw that my students made poor choices about sources in their argumentative essays, so I focused a few social bookmarking activities on finding credible sources.

3. Explore ways that technology can capture student thinking in the moment and in the space where it's happening. Maybe that means using a classroom response system or small whiteboards to identify student misconceptions during class, or perhaps that means leveraging student mobile devices and apps to surface student learning outside of class. You might find yourself learning about student perspectives that ordinarily aren't shared.

4. Create safe spaces for students to take risks and to share their perspectives honestly. If you really want to know where students are struggling in their learning, you have to give them permission to share something that's not correct or fully fleshed out. This might mean giving students a way to respond anonymously to a question, or at least a venue where other students don't know who said what.

5. When setting up formative assessment, practice *light grading*.[17] Instead of evaluating the quality of a student tweet or bookmark or whiteboard diagram, grade on effort, grade generously, or don't grade at all. If the stakes are too high, students will stop taking risks and you won't find out what they're really thinking. And grading on effort is usually fine for these kinds of activities, since students receive feedback on the learning they exhibit through mechanisms other than grades, like class discussion.

6. To provide students feedback, practice agile teaching. That is, use what you learn about your students through formative assessment to inform what and how you teach. In some

cases, this means responding to individual students to help them with particular problems. In other cases, this means responding in an aggregate way to trends and themes you see in student work. What you find out about student learning through formative assessment should change what happens in your classroom.

7. Be prepared to be surprised. If it's your first time using a particular activity, you may find out that some of your other instructional activities aren't as effective as you thought they were. Even when you've used a particular formative assessment repeatedly, every group of students you work with is different. The class in front of you may have very different misconceptions or perspectives than the class last semester—or even earlier in the day.

8. Consider both open-ended prompts and more structured assessments. Open-ended prompts ask more of students and have more potential to reveal things about student learning you didn't know. But if you have a hunch about where student misconceptions lie or don't have the time to read through a lot of responses to an open-ended prompt, a multiple-choice question or similarly structured prompt can still be very useful at showing trends in student thinking.

9. Mix up your media. Tracy Ruscetti asks her students to draw concept maps illustrating their understanding. Ashley Hasty asks her students to talk about their visual design choices. Margaret Rubega encourages her students to tweet photos of birds they spot. In my workshops on teaching, I'll often ask participants to submit a *visual minute paper* at the end—a doodle representing one thing they heard at the workshop that they want to try in their teaching. Often moving into a medium other than straight text can reveal different aspects of learning.

10. Create all-skate experiences. If you ask students a question and two students respond with good answers, you've learned nothing about the other students in the room. Try

out technologies and strategies that make lots of students' learning visible, not just the learning of a handful of students. If you have a large class, consider tools that aggregate student responses in some way or give the collected responses back to your students for analysis.

We can't actually see our students learning; that all happens inside their brains. But if we're clever and intentional, we can design forms of assessment (maybe even new forms) that help us understand that learning through what our students write and draw and say and create. And that understanding can inform our work as we help them navigate that "intermediate space between novice and expert" where learning happens.

CHAPTER 4

Knowledge Organizations

IMAGINE YOU HAVE a couple thousand books in your personal library. Books on all kinds of topics, written by all kinds of authors. Imagine also you have a beautiful room in your house to keep all these books, a room with floor-to-ceiling shelves. You could arrange your books on those shelves by topic or by author or by the Library of Congress Classification or by the Dewey Decimal System. Instead, however, you decide to arrange your personal library . . . by the color of each book's spine. Your library is a rainbow, with red and orange books to your left as you enter the room, blending to yellow and green books over your comfy couch, turning into blue and purple books to the right of the bay window. You love having friends over, just so you can show them your rainbow library.

Wouldn't that be beautiful? It's a life goal of mine to own enough books to pull this off. Sure, there are other organization schemes that would be more informative or efficient, but there's some level of practicality in a rainbow library. Over time, one would learn to associate particular books with their colors, so that finding a book would get faster and faster. It's certainly a better organizational scheme than keeping books in random piles all around the library. In a random-pile library, it would take forever to find a particular book. For a library to be functional, it needs some kind of organization (even if it's by color), and a better organizational scheme can result in a more functional library.

That's also true for the knowledge we have in our heads. We can't help but organize the facts, examples, concepts, and techniques we know (or think we know) in some way. Cognitive scientists call these ways of grouping and connecting and sorting what we know *knowledge organizations*. The better a person's knowledge organization, the better equipped the person is to access their knowledge and use it to answer questions and solve problems. Consider the visualizations of novice and expert knowledge organizations in figure 7, adapted from illustrations in Susan Ambrose and colleagues' *How Learning Works*.

In the visualizations (which are, mathematically speaking, graphs) in figure 7, each node represents some bit of knowledge—a concept, an example, a procedure, an argument. The lines between nodes

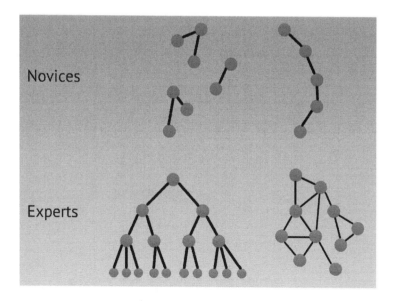

Figure 7. Visualizations of knowledge organizations, adapted from *How Learning Works*.

represent associations or connections among the corresponding bits of knowledge. For example, you might have nodes for the city Nashville, the state Tennessee, and the concept of "state capitals," with links between Nashville and Tennessee (because Nashville is a city in Tennessee) and between Nashville and "state capitals" (because Nashville is a state capital).

Novices in a particular domain tend to have fairly sparse knowledge organizations. There aren't many nodes (because the novice hasn't learned many concepts or examples or skills yet), and those nodes aren't well connected. Sometimes a novice will have a few bits of (thus far) unrelated information. Other times, a novice will have a very linear approach to the domain. I see this in mathematics sometimes when students are good at following mathematical "recipes" but aren't able to solve problems that don't look just like the ones in the textbook.

Experts, on the other hand, have much more robust knowledge organizations. There are more nodes, more connections between nodes, and those connections are more meaningful. Sometimes an expert will organize their knowledge hierarchically, sometimes less so. Regardless, an expert's knowledge organization helps them quickly retrieve information that's relevant to the case at hand, make sense of new information by "slotting" it into their existing knowledge organization, and, as a result, respond adaptively to solve problems they have never seen before.[1]

Building robust knowledge organizations isn't easy, just as changing mental models of individual concepts isn't easy. When students in an introductory course open up their textbooks for the first time, they encounter a host of new terms and examples and stories. Until they start to understand the relationships between topics, they can't see the forest for the trees. Part of our role as instructors is to help students see the big picture in our courses. This leads to our next principle of teaching.

PRINCIPLE 4. *Providing students with visual ways to organize their knowledge can help them remember and use that knowledge.*

If we want to help our students develop expertise and thus become better problem solvers, then we need to help them expand and refine their knowledge organizations. Some instructional practices are more useful for this than others, and some technologies, both digital and analog, are more useful than others.

How a Mathematician Teaches a Novel

In the introduction to this book, I mentioned that not all educational technology is digital in nature. That's certainly true for the story I'm about to share, in which the technology I used consisted of large Post-it notes and good markers. I have a theory that most of the world's problems could be solved if enough creative people got together with enough Post-it notes and markers.

As I mentioned in an earlier chapter, my cryptography seminar is an unusual course, with code-making and code-breaking, pure mathematics, history, current events, and writing instruction. If that wasn't enough, I also teach a novel. I can assure you, teaching novels was not something covered in my graduate seminar on teaching mathematics. The novel I teach is Cory Doctor's *Little Brother*, in which teenage hacker Marcus Yallow and his friends fight against increasingly aggressive surveillance by the Department of Homeland Security after a major act of terrorism. The novel is an engaging read, and it tackles one of the key questions we explore in the seminar: how should we balance security and privacy in a digital world? That's a tough question with a complex answer, one that's part of our national discourse now, thanks to Edward Snowden. Learning to write about complex issues is one of the goals of the seminar, so I've developed an in-class activity using *Little Brother* to help students make sense of the complex security versus privacy debate, as a precursor to writing assignments on this theme later in the semester. In the activity, I ask students to construct what I call a *debate map*.

After having read (and blogged about) *Little Brother* before class, the students start class by working in groups of three to identify two pro-security arguments and two pro-privacy arguments made by characters in the novel. I distribute large Post-it notes (five by seven inches each) to the students along with a few markers. I ask the students to summarize the arguments they identified on the Post-it notes, with pro-security arguments on notes of one color and pro-privacy arguments on notes of another color. Each Post-it note is to include the name of the character making the argument, along with the corresponding page number in the novel. The students jump right into this work, some groups moving more quickly than others to fill their Post-it notes but all groups digging into the novel to find arguments on either side of the issue. The room usually gets a little noisy at this point, with fifteen students all talking at once. During this time, I circulate among the students, answering questions and making sure groups are staying on task.

That's phase one. For phase two, I have the groups take turns sharing an argument they identified with the class and posting it on the chalkboard. I ask students to place more practically focused arguments ("Is all this surveillance really catching terrorists?") at one end of the board and more principled arguments ("It's life, liberty, and the pursuit of happiness, in that order.") at the other end. I also ask them to connect their argument to one or more other arguments already on the board, drawing an arrow in chalk to represent those connections. For example, a new argument might support one already on the board or counter a different argument already posted.

Groups make their contributions one at a time, with each group sending a representative to the board to place a Post-it note and summarize the argument it represents. The first couple of contributions are often a bit hesitant, as it isn't entirely clear to students which arguments are more practical in nature and which are more about principles, nor is it clear how one argument might connect to another. I will step in and make some suggestions ("That sounds like a fairly practical argument" or "Your argument seems to support this other argument"), and soon enough the students get the hang of it and are adding their arguments to the board in sensible ways. To see what the finished debate map looked like in the 2015 offering of the course, see figure 8.

Having taught this first-year writing seminar a few times, I've learned that most of my students can argue one side of a debate, but

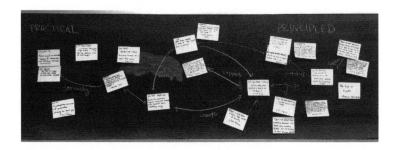

Figure 8. Finished *Little Brother* debate map from 2015. Photo by Derek Bruff.

many struggle to do so in a way that acknowledges the complexity of the debate. For instance, they have a hard time raising potential objections to their arguments and offering compelling counterarguments to those objections. This debate map activity prepares them to do that by helping them see how arguments interact with each other.

The visual thinking in the activity helps students expand and refine their own knowledge organizations. As they work in groups and as a whole class to map out the security-privacy debate as it is reflected in the novel, they see on the chalkboard how key ideas and arguments in this debate connect with each other. This gives them the opportunity to build these arguments and relationships into their own understandings of the debate. To help this process along, I ask them to spend some time as a class evaluating the debate map and discussing the arguments they find most surprising or compelling or frustrating. This in turn prepares them for future assignments, including a research-based argumentative essay on the security-privacy debate I assign later in the semester.

As I noted above, this is a low-tech activity. That wasn't always the case, however. The first time I ran this activity, I had students construct the debate map in Prezi, a useful presentation tool and perhaps an even better mind-mapping tool. Since Prezi allows for multiple editors on the same presentations, I had students make their contributions to a shared digital debate map as they worked in small groups. This got a little chaotic, with students adding arguments on top of each other and at dramatically different font sizes. By switching to Post-it notes on a chalkboard, I was able to better control the timing of the activity, asking students to add arguments sequentially, instead of concurrently, and to help shape the structure of the debate map. As a result, when it was time to step back and evaluate the debate map, the students weren't trying to make heads or tails of the map. Instead, they already understood how it was put together.

Making sure students understand the visual heuristics they are using is an important part of activities like this one, as visualizations of knowledge organizations can look pretty messy and thus be confusing. If you're going to have students make use of a complex visualization, they'll need to understand how it works. And having them take their time to create the visualization is one way to help them achieve that understanding. I could have shown my students a well-developed security-privacy debate map, instead of having them go through the process of creating their own relatively small debate map. However, just viewing a complete debate map doesn't help students build out their own knowledge organizations to the same extent that building a debate map from scratch does. The process here matters more than the final product.

Although the debate map activity itself was low-tech, there was a digital technology piece to the 2015 debate map experience for my students. After class, I blogged about the activity, then tweeted a link to the blog post, tagging the author of *Little Brother*, Cory Doctorow, in the tweet. I knew he was active on Twitter, and there was a chance he would notice the tweet. Not only did he notice the tweet, but he also wrote about my blog post on his popular blog *Boing Boing*. I started the next class session by pulling up his blog post on the big screen and enjoying my students' reactions as they realized the author of the novel they had just read blogged about the debate map they created to represent his novel![2]

The engagement didn't stop there, however. I had noticed that Cory Doctorow framed the debate map as surveillance vs. privacy, not security vs. privacy as I had framed it. Back on Twitter, I asked him about the word choice, and he responded with a series of tweets on the topic.[3] During class, after showing my students his blog post,

I pointed out his word choice (surveillance instead of security) and asked my students what they thought about it. We had a lively discussion before I shared with them Doctorow's comments on Twitter. They were, again, surprised to see the author of the book they had just read fielding questions about our class activity! This sequence had a time for telling element, too, since students were primed to make sense of Doctorow's response by the conversation I had with them.

Even better, the students were very intentional about how they defined and used the terms *security* and *surveillance* the rest of the semester, including in their argumentative essays later in the course. I don't think that would have happened without the interactions with the author made possible by social media. As we'll see in chapter 7, digital technology can be helpful in connecting our students with wider audiences—including the authors of the texts they are studying.

For the security and privacy discussion in my cryptography seminar, a debate map was the right visualization tool to help students grapple with the complexity of that discussion and develop their own knowledge organizations of the topic. Debate maps are useful in a variety of teaching contexts—see, for instance, Christine D'Onofrio's use of a debate map to explore the concept of appropriation in her visual arts class.[4] Sometimes, however, other kinds of visualization tools are a better fit. A good visualization tool, with some appropriate technology and a useful process, can help students see the big picture in a course, as well as how details fit into that big picture, which helps students build out their internal knowledge organizations. Many such visualization tools fall in the loose category of "maps." Following are examples from a few disciplines of mapping approaches to enhance knowledge organization development.

Multiscale Mapping

Cynthia Brame teaches biology at Vanderbilt University. (She also has an office right down the hall from me, since we both work at the Vanderbilt Center for Teaching.) Although I had some trouble using Prezi for my debate map activity, she found the zooming presentation tool a good fit for an assignment in her course on the biology of cancer.

She asked her students to create what she called *synthesis maps*, visual representations of their understandings of carcinogenesis (cancer formation). These synthesis maps not only provided the students opportunities to expand and refine their own knowledge organizations, but they also provided Brame with insight into her students' learning.

Prezi allows users to arrange text, images, and videos on a blank digital canvas and, key to the synthesis map assignment, zoom into that canvas to embed content at different scales. Brame asked her students, a mix of junior and senior science and engineering majors, to use Prezi to create visualizations of their evolving understandings of how cancer works. Students created initial synthesis maps during the third week of the course, representing what relatively limited knowledge they had of cancer at the time visually on their Prezi canvases. Students received feedback on their initial synthesis maps from their instructor and from their peers. They revised and expanded their synthesis maps three more times during the course, incorporating what they had learned in the course and receiving more peer and instructor feedback on each iteration.

By the end of the semester, students had created visually rich representations of their own understandings of the biology of cancer. See figures 9 and 10 for screenshots from a synthesis map created by Brame's student, John Cao, for a sense of how these maps can work, and view the online version to explore Cao's entire map.[5]

Brame worked with Ryan Ortega, a biomedical engineering graduate student, to analyze her students' synthesis maps after the course was complete.[6] They considered the different ways students organized their maps (conceptual, spatial, or narrative), and scored the maps on a number of criteria, including organization between major concepts, organization within major concepts, completeness, and accuracy. Those four criteria yielded a total score for each synthesis map. Brame and Ortega also considered a map's embeddedness, that is, the highest number of times the synthesis map nested some piece of content inside other content. (Think of it as an *Inception* score.)

Among other findings, Brame and Ortega determined that a map's embeddedness was significantly correlated with the map's total score, indicating that students with better understandings of carcinogenesis

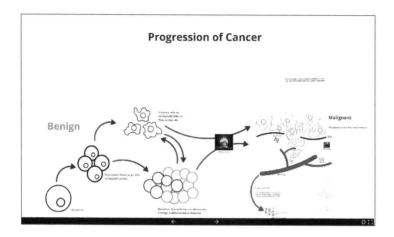

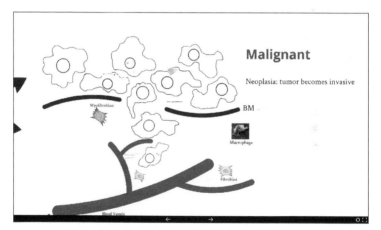

Figure 9 (*top*). Screenshot of John Cao's synthesis map, zoom level one.

Figure 10 (*bottom*). Screenshot of John Cao's synthesis map, zoom level two.

concepts and processes tended to use Prezi's zooming features more robustly to represent that understanding. They also observed a significant correlation between a student's final exam score in the course and that student's map's score on organization between major concepts, indicating that the synthesis maps enhanced, or at least reflected, a student's big-picture understanding in the course. Brame and Ortega's analysis yielded other results, but these two results illustrate one reason I like sharing this example: the affordances of the technology Brame used (the visualization tools provided by Prezi) were a good match for the kinds of thinking she wanted her students to do (refining their knowledge organizations by making sense of cancer concepts and relationships among those concepts). Brame and Ortega say much the same in their paper: "One of the challenges in understanding a complex process like carcinogenesis is fitting the different components into a coherent whole. By constructing visual representations of their [mental] model (which, by definition, changes in response to new knowledge), the students clarified and structured their growing understanding of carcinogenesis."[7]

Although there was a good match between technology and pedagogy here, the technology brought with it certain challenges. As noted, students who more frequently used Prezi's zooming feature tended to have better synthesis maps. However, the zooming feature isn't the most intuitive part of Prezi. Brame recommends that instructors interested in synthesis maps assignments using Prezi show their students examples of what one can do with Prezi's zooming feature to help them understand how they could use the feature effectively.

More generally, Brame recommends that instructors provide students with a fair amount of instruction and support on the front end of this kind of assignment. For many students, using Prezi is a new skill, so some orientation is warranted. Also new territory for many students: representing their own understanding through visualization tools like synthesis maps. The iterative process Brame used, having students revise and expand their synthesis maps three times during the semester, with feedback each time, provided useful opportunities for students to get better at constructing synthesis maps.

Intersecting Lives

Georgetown University's Sarah Stiles had her students create maps in Prezi as well, but different kinds of maps for a different kind of course. As with my debate map activity, sociology professor Stiles had her students find connections within a text, but her activity featured a nonfiction work, *Ain't No Makin' It: Aspirations and Attainment in a Low-Income Neighborhood* by Jay MacLeod. The book is an ethnography that tracks the lives of two groups of young men—one mostly black, one mostly white—in a public housing development in Massachusetts in the 1980s and early 1990s, and Stiles assigned it as a reading in her Contemporary City course as a way to explore social reproduction theory.

Stiles wanted her students to see and understand the connections and relationships among the characters in the book and to situate the characters' experiences on a common timeline. (I use the term *character* here, but the individuals described in the book are actual people.) Prezi's multimedia editing features gave her students a useful set of tools for describing the personal histories of the young men in the ethnography. To help students learn to use Prezi, she first assigned individual character presentations, in which each student was given a character and asked to design a presentation focused on that character. This assignment gave each student a chance to see what could be done in the tool to represent a character and their experiences.

Following the individual character presentations, Stiles split her students into two groups of seven students each and assigned each group one of the groups of young men in the text, the Hallway Hangers and the Brothers. The group task was to map out the stories of the young men on a shared Prezi canvas using an image of a timeline provided by Stiles, with the Hallway Hangers represented above the timeline and the Brothers below. Each group appointed an editor who added material to the shared Prezi, but all group members contributed ideas, descriptions, and images. The groups then presented their maps to each other, using Prezi's presentation mode to walk through the maps they had made.

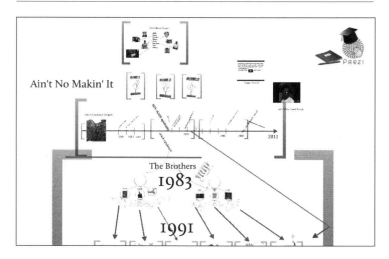

Figure 11. Screenshot of *Ain't No Making It* character map by Sarah Stiles' students.

Given the editing process used to construct it, the resulting character map (fig. 11) is remarkably coherent. Both groups of students used tree diagrams to describe their characters, and both groups used Prezi's zooming features to embed information drawn from and complementary to the text at different scales. In a blog post about the activity, Yong Lee notes that these visual heuristics were adopted by the students on the fly during class with relatively little discussion, perhaps because tree diagrams were used in the individual character maps shared at the start of the group activity.[8] Lee also notes that requiring each group to appoint a single editor not only helped the online tool run more smoothly (since only a couple of students were editing concurrently) but also fostered a helpful consensus-building process among the student groups.

Stiles describes the activity as "very successful for the students." One reason is that it helped the students understand the young men from the ethnography in context. For instance, when crack cocaine hit the streets in the eighties, it had a significant effect on some of the young men. Some avoided the drug, while it led others to spiral down. In another case, a building boom in Florida led one character to move there for a job, which led to a pretty good life there. In both instances, mapping historical events on the same timeline as the personal narratives of the young men helped Stiles's students see how social changes affect individual lives in different ways. This, in turn, helped the students better understand social reproduction theory, which was Stiles's overall learning goal for this part of the course.

Near and Far

Earlier I described how a mathematician (me) teaches a novel using a debate map. Do actual English professors use any kind of mapping techniques with students when teaching novels? Yes! And sometimes they even use actual maps.

In 2011 Erin Sells, then a visiting assistant professor of English at Lander University, shared a post on the blog *ProfHacker* describing her students' use of Google Earth to map the Virginia Woolf novel *Mrs. Dalloway*.[9] Like my debate map activity, Sells's assignment involved group work and whole-class collaboration. Like Cynthia Brame's synthesis map assignment, Sells's students created multimedia-rich maps. And like Sarah Stiles's Prezi activity, Sells had her students map the experiences of characters in the text at hand. Unlike those other activities, however, Sells's mapping activity involved real-world geospatial data.

Sells assigned one of the four major characters in the novel (including the titular Mrs. Dalloway) to each of four groups of students in her course. Each group tracked their character through the novel, identified physical locations in London visited by or referenced by their character, and mapped their character's narrative arc through London using Google Earth, annotating their character's journey with text, images, sounds, and videos. Each group presented their maps to the class, then the four maps were combined into a single Google Earth map of the entire novel (fig. 12). Sells then explored with her students what the intersections seen in the combined map revealed about the characters and the novel.

In her *ProfHacker* post, Sells mentions some of the aha moments her students had constructing their maps. For example, one group

Figure 12. Screenshot of *Mrs. Dalloway* novel map by Erin Sells' students.

was surprised to discover just how far across London the character Peter Walsh follows a young woman he has his eye on, providing insight into the intensity of Walsh's interest in the young woman. Another group realized that their character, Elizabeth Dalloway, traveled across London along routes that her mother would never choose to take, again revealing something about that character. In each case, the process of mapping characters' movements geographically revealed aspects of the novel the students had not previously understood. These revelations were identified by students in the reflection papers Sells asked them to write after completing the assignment.

Apparently, mapping and Virginia Woolf go well together because Amanda Golden also asked her students to map a Woolf novel. As a postdoctoral fellow at the Georgia Institute of Technology, Golden taught a course called "Digital Woolf" in Georgia Tech's writing and communication program. That program emphasizes multimodal communication through their WOVEN framework (Written, Oral, Visual, Electronic, and Nonverbal), and Golden's assignment incorporated several aspects of that framework.[10] She had her students use mapping and presentation tools, including Google Maps, PowerPoint, and

Prezi, to map sections of Woolf's 1922 novel *Jacob's Room*, then share those maps with the whole class.

As Golden writes, "As we began reading *Jacob's Room*, the students found it incomprehensible."[11] One reason is that the novel focuses more on "sensory perceptions" than traditional forms of plot and character development. Many of the places mentioned in the novel aren't places visited by the characters but are instead places characters think about or imagine. By asking students to map these places, Golden helped her students practice a form of close reading of the novel, making sense of the sometimes cryptic prose by looking for and analyzing places and locations referenced in the text, not unlike the close reading done by Kathryn Tomasek's history students.

Golden and her students mapped the fifth chapter of *Jacob's Room* together during class. Then she had groups of students tackle different chapters of the novel to create their own maps (fig. 13). They found different ways to represent their assigned chapters visually using the tools at hand. One group used color to distinguish between actual places visited by characters and those places only imagined by characters. Another used lines and paths to visualize "virtual lines of sight" where characters thought about the central character Jacob. Another group realized that the short, final chapter could be represented with just a handful of marks on a map, showing just how small and insignificant the supposedly central character of Jacob really was.

Golden, now an English professor at New York Institute of Technology, continues to use mapping tools to help students make sense of texts. For instance, in her Global Digital Modernisms course, she has students map *Good Morning, Midnight*, a 1938 novel by Jean Rhys. As with *Jacob's Room*, her students find this novel hard to read thanks to the stream-of-consciousness approach it takes, and they often don't like it when they first encounter it. Mapping the novel, then viewing their classmates' maps helps her students make sense of and appreciate the novel. In fact, Golden says that mapping techniques work best with difficult novels. She finds that if the novel is too straightforward, students simply plot places and character movements. For more challenging, impressionist novels, the mapping process provides students a mechanism for important sense-making.

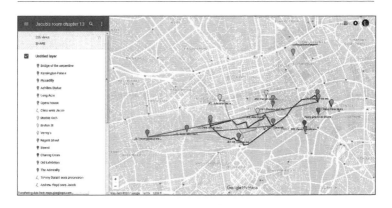

Figure 13. Screenshot of *Jacob's Room* novel map by Amanda Golden's students.

Since mapping novels using tools like Google Maps or Prezi is often a new kind of learning task for her students, Golden finds it useful to provide her students with several examples of maps. Without such examples, she finds that some students aren't sure how to go about these mapping activities. When she shares examples, some students see them and take very similar approaches to their own maps. Other students, however, use the example maps as inspiration for their own creative takes on mapping novels. For instance, student Tia Widianto created a map in Prezi that layers a period map of Paris with text and image annotations (fig. 14). Golden also provides plenty of opportunities for in-class mapping, often through smaller mapping projects, so that she can model the process for students and assist them as they start trying to map things.

In the case of both of these instructors, the geospatial maps of novels created by students helped students uncover and understand relationships and themes in the novels they read, refining their own big-picture understandings of the novels. As Sells writes, "The map itself is just a starting point—as layers of information into the sights and sounds of the city on this summer day in London are added, it becomes a multi-dimensional research project and gives students a guide to navigating a difficult novel."

The mapping approaches to building student knowledge

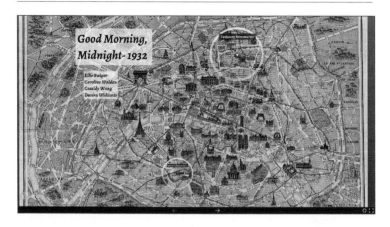

Figure 14. Screenshot of *Good Morning, Midnight* novel map by student Tia Widianto.

organizations described above are all somewhat open-ended. That is, students are generally able to decide how they want to visually arrange information on the maps they create. Sometimes, however, more structure is useful in helping students see connections and relationships among concepts and examples in a course, as the next two stories illustrate.

Up, Down, Left, Right

There was a day when a timeline was a simple linear arrangement of events by date, a static visualization perhaps printed on a two-page spread in a textbook. However, today's digital timelines are interactive and allow for the use of text, images, sound, and video, using spatial arrangements and color schemes to convey meaning.

While teaching religious studies at Vanderbilt University, Bryan Lowe participated in a Center for Teaching learning community on the use of digital timelines in teaching, and he found digital timelines to be a useful solution to a particular teaching problem of his. Lowe teaches a Religions of Japan course that covers two thousand years of religious history, from early myths to modern practices. Lowe wants the students in this entry-level undergraduate course to learn to think both *diachronically* and *synchronically*. That is, he wants students to identify and analyze historical trajectories, finding connections among ideas, movements, and themes across time (diachronically), and he wants students to understand that religious traditions are always embedded in historical, political, and cultural contexts of the time they exist (synchronically). Instead of teaching this survey course in the usual chronological fashion, moving from the premodern era to today, Lowe has arranged the course thematically. This helps his students think diachronically, as they examine trends and themes in Japanese religious thought over time, but it can make it challenging for students to think synchronically. Lowe says, "In putting early myths, medieval tales, ethnography, and modern films in dialogue, students often forget context."[12] They lose the chronology, and they fail to grasp how historical moments influence theology and practice.

To counteract this, Lowe asked his students to create digital timelines using the online tool Tiki-Toki. Each student created their own timeline and were assigned to add four entries to their timeline each week of the course. Each entry, drawn from the course readings, Lowe's lectures, or additional research by the students, consisted of a title, description, date or date range, citation, and, when appropriate, some kind of media, such as an image or video. Each entry was also assigned to one of four categories: people, texts, beliefs and practices, and historical context. Tiki-Toki makes it relatively easy to create timelines of this sort, with a variety of visual organization schemes that leverage the categories used within a timeline.

For instance, consider the four different views of the same timeline created by student Patrick Meng (figs. 15, 16, 17, and 18).[13] Tiki-Toki calls these views standard, category bands, duration, and colored stories. These different views give students tools for thinking about their timelines diachronically or synchronically.

By the end of the course, each student had a timeline with more than fifty entries. Students received some credit just for completing their entries, but the timeline entries were also graded on accuracy, depth of information, use of media, quality of writing, and citations. Students were given written feedback on their timelines twice during

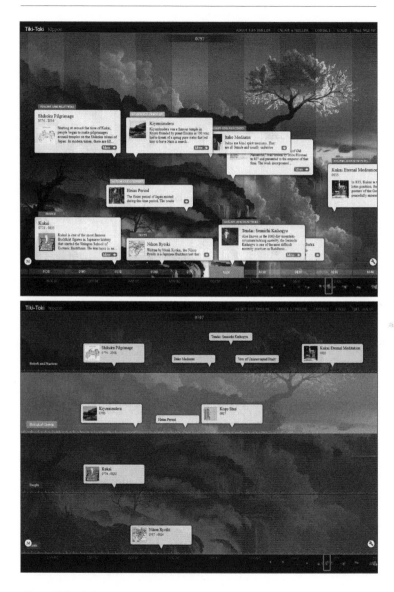

Figure 15 (*top*). Screenshot of Patrick Meng's "Nippon" timeline, standard view.

Figure 16 (*bottom*). Screenshot of Patrick Meng's "Nippon" timeline, category view.

Figure 17 (*top*). Screenshot of Patrick Meng's "Nippon" timeline, duration view.

Figure 18 (*bottom*). Screenshot of Patrick Meng's "Nippon" timeline, stories view.

the semester before final grading. Students also presented their timelines in progress during class during the semester, for additional infor-
mal feedback. Finally, Lowe asked his students to write an analytical
paper at the end of the course responding to one of four prompts.
Each student had to draw on their timeline to write their paper and
include a paragraph explaining how they did so.

Lowe's goal with the timeline assignment was to help his students
think not just diachronically but also synchronically, and he points
to evidence that the assignment was successful in this. For instance,
one student considered attitudes toward spirits of the dead over time,
reporting that "she learned to recognize how all new ideas are 'formed
with a purpose' bound to the historical context in which they developed." Another student "compared doctrines from contemporaneous
texts from different sectarian traditions to show a cross-fertilization
of ideas across Buddhist sects active at the same time."[14] The timeline
assignment proved a useful complement to Lowe's thematic organization of the course, and the visualization scheme and interactive tools
provided by Tiki-Toki helped students see relationships both within
and across time periods.[15]

On the Grid

I teach a course in linear algebra at Vanderbilt from time to time. The
course starts with a unit on systems of linear equations. Remember
back in high school algebra when you had to find the values of x and
y that worked for a pair of equations like $4x + 5y = 10$ and $3x - 2y = 6$?
Those are linear equations, and when you have more than one of them,
you have a system of linear equations. In the first unit, we look at such
systems and we ask three important questions about them: Given a
system of linear equations, does the system have a solution (existence)? If so, is that solution unique or is there more than one solution
(uniqueness)? And can the system be solved for any possible set of
constant terms (consistency)?

Any system of linear equation can also be represented as something called a vector equation and something else called a matrix
equation. And those three questions we ask about linear equations

can be restated to apply to vector equations and matrix equations. A lot of linear algebra problems involve taking a mathematical model posed in one context (say, a system of equations derived from some word problem), translating it into another context (perhaps a matrix equation), using some mathematical tools to answer the question in the new context (maybe row-reducing the matrix), then translating the answer back to the original context.

That's not at all obvious when we start the course.

In fact, a few weeks into the course, most students still don't get that big picture. I'm not sure I did, either, until I had taught the course once through! But once a student understands that's what is happening—three questions, multiple contexts, different tools within each context to answer those questions—they are able to tackle a variety of problems in linear algebra with confidence and success. To help my students see that big picture, I designed a series of in-class activities based on a graphic organizer I call a *representation grid*.

As a review activity before the first exam, I distributed paper copies of a handout (table 1). The grid has a row for each context (linear, vector, and matrix equations) and a column for each of the three big questions (existence, uniqueness, consistency). Most of the grid is blank. It is the student's job to translate those three big questions from one context to the other. I set up the grid Sudoku-style, where there's just enough information given for students to fill in the rest of the grid. I asked my students to work in pairs to complete the grid, then had pairs take turns contributing their answers to a version of the grid I drew on the chalkboard at the front of the room.

During the review session before the second exam, we built on our earlier work. By this point in the course, we had added subspaces and linear transformations as two additional contexts for the three big questions, so I added rows for those and had the students complete the expanded grid (table 2). Like Cynthia Brame with her synthesis map activity, I saw value in having students add to their big-picture visualization at multiple points during the course. And, importantly, I didn't just give my students a completed grid to use as a study aid.

Context	Example	Visualization	Question 1	Question 2	Question 3
Systems of Linear Equations	Solve $2x_1 - 3x_2 = 4,$ $x_1 + 5x_2 = 3.$				Is the system consistent for all possible right hand sides?
Vector Equations		Head-to-tail addition of scaled vectors			
Matrix Equations		None	Is $\begin{bmatrix} 4 \\ 3 \end{bmatrix}$ a linear combination of the columns of A?		
To Answer:	Not applicable	Not applicable		Row-reduce the coefficient matrix. Check for free variables.	

Table 1. Representation grid for first linear algebra review session, to be completed.

I asked them to try completing a grid before I shared my "expert" version, creating a time for telling.

This was a low-tech activity, using just handouts and the chalkboard, but the goal wasn't to create a collaborative or multimedia document. The goal was to have students start to organize their understanding of the main ideas in the course. Where a map or a timeline might serve that purpose in another context, here a well-structured grid seemed most appropriate. And analog can be a useful approach for building knowledge organizations. As noted in the first chapter, there's some evidence that digital games are less useful than analog games for teaching systems thinking.[16] There might be something about the small screen of a phone that makes it harder for learners to see relationships and make connections. It's likely more useful to use a visualization where students can see the entire picture at once, like the analog visualizations mentioned in this chapter, or structure the visualization activity so that students are actively engaged in building the visualization, not just viewing it.

Context	Example	Visualization	Question 1	Question 2	Question 3
Systems of Linear Equations	Solve $2x_1 - 3x_2 = 4$, $x_1 + 5x_2 = 3$.	Intersecting lines, planes, and so on	Is the system consistent?	If so, is the solution unique?	Is the system consistent for all possible right hand sides?
Vector Equations	Solve $x_1 \begin{bmatrix} 2 \\ 1 \end{bmatrix} + x_2 \begin{bmatrix} -3 \\ 5 \end{bmatrix} = \begin{bmatrix} 4 \\ 3 \end{bmatrix}$.	Head-to-tail addition of scaled vectors	Is $\begin{bmatrix} 4 \\ 3 \end{bmatrix}$ a linear combo of $\begin{bmatrix} 2 \\ 1 \end{bmatrix}$ and $\begin{bmatrix} -3 \\ 5 \end{bmatrix}$?	Are the vectors $\begin{bmatrix} 2 \\ 1 \end{bmatrix}$ and $\begin{bmatrix} -3 \\ 5 \end{bmatrix}$ linearly independent?	Do the vectors $\begin{bmatrix} 2 \\ 1 \end{bmatrix}$ and $\begin{bmatrix} -3 \\ 5 \end{bmatrix}$ span $\mathbb{R}^2$?
Matrix Equations	Solve $Ax = \begin{bmatrix} 4 \\ 3 \end{bmatrix}$ where $A = \begin{bmatrix} 2 & -3 \\ 1 & 5 \end{bmatrix}$.	None	Is $\begin{bmatrix} 4 \\ 3 \end{bmatrix}$ a linear combination of the columns of A?	Are the columns of A linearly independent?	Do the columns of A span $\mathbb{R}^2$?
Subspaces	Consider $A = \begin{bmatrix} 2 & -3 \\ 1 & 5 \end{bmatrix}$ and $\mathbf{x} = \begin{bmatrix} 4 \\ 3 \end{bmatrix}$.	Points, lines, planes, and so on			
Linear Transformations	Let $T : \mathbb{R}^2 \to \mathbb{R}^2$ have standard matrix $\begin{bmatrix} 2 & -3 \\ 1 & 5 \end{bmatrix}$.	Reflections, rotations, and so on (for some transformations)			
To Answer:	Not applicable	Not applicable	Row-reduce the augmented matrix. Look for a row of all zeros except for a nonzero entry in the rightmost column.	Row-reduce the augmented matrix. Check for free variables.	Row-reduce the coefficient matrix. Check for a row of all zeros.

Table 2. Representation grid for second linear algebra review session, to be completed.

Practical Advice

As you consider ways to use technology to help students expand and refine their knowledge organizations, keep in the mind the following suggestions.

1. Instead of sharing a visualization you've created with your students, ask them to (co-)create a visualization themselves. Making sense of someone else's knowledge organization can be useful, but it's often more useful for students to visualize their own knowledge organization, then use that visualization to expand and refine their knowledge organization.
2. Provide students with example visualizations, or have them construct simple ones as practice. Constructing these kinds of

visualizations is usually a new experience for students, with or without technology, so they'll need some scaffolding. For instance, you might build part of a visualization together as a class, then have students work on their own or in groups to expand or complete it.

3. Similarly, students might not get why you're asking them to create visualizations, especially if you're using a visualization technique that's not standard in your discipline. You'll want to explain to students why you're assigning the activity and what you hope they gain from it. And after they complete the activity, you might need to point out to them what they learned from it.

4. Match your visual heuristic to the content or your learning goals. For some activities, a free-form mind map might be most useful; for others, a more structured grid of some kind might work best. You might even combine the two approaches, as I did with my debate map. Most of the map was organic, but I added a horizontal axis (from practical to principled arguments) to provide some structure.

5. Explore a variety of visual heuristics to create meaning for students. You might ask students to cluster examples that are like each other, place examples on a continuum, build a flowchart, or use color to categorize examples. See *The Visual Display of Quantitative Information* by Edward Tufte or *The Back of the Napkin* by Dan Roam for inspiration.[17]

6. Consider having students work in groups to create or contribute to a visualization. Sometimes solo work is a good way for students to get started, but having students collaborate, even in pairs, can help them engage more actively with a visualization. Requiring a group of students to come to a consensus about their contribution can motivate healthy debate and discussion.

7. Once students have constructed a visualization, have them spend some time analyzing it or reflecting on the process they used to create the visualization. That is, don't let the visualization be the end of the learning process but use it as a tool

for deeper learning. You might have students make sense of their own individual visualization, review and provide feedback on a peer's visualization, or use a collaboratively constructed class visualization in a later assignment.

8. Ask students to revisit their visualizations later in the course, perhaps revising or expanding them to account for new concepts and examples. Creating a visualization once will likely help students develop their mental knowledge organizations. Returning to the same visualization repeatedly will do even more to help them internalize the big picture.

9. Be mindful of the learning curve of any visualization technology you use. For instance, it can be useful to have students add media (images, sounds, videos) to a map or timeline, but figuring out how to do so might be challenging depending on the tool used. Sometimes, a simpler or low-tech approach is better, particularly for a one-off visualization activity.

10. Perhaps most importantly, don't ask students to map out the big picture if your goal for a class session or activity is to focus on details, especially in isolation. Sometimes students need practice with a single concept or skill, in which case some other form of activity is more appropriate. See chapter 2 on practice and feedback for ideas.

These kinds of activities might not be appropriate for every class session, but it is important to occasionally direct students to the big picture in a course. As Ambrose and colleagues write in *How Learning Works*, "When students are provided with an organizational structure in which to fit new knowledge, they learn more effectively and efficiently than when they are left to deduce this conceptual structure for themselves."[18]

CHAPTER 5

Multimodal Assignments

LEARNING STYLES don't exist.

There, I said it.

When I make this statement at workshops, I always pause for a reaction. Sometimes I get angry looks; other times, cheering and applause. There's almost always some kind of reaction.

That's because a lot of educators have heard about learning styles, and a lot of educators believe that learning styles provide a useful framework for making instructional choices. Specifically, they believe in what's known as the *matching hypothesis*. This is the notion that when we match our instructional methods to a student's preferred way of learning, the student learns better. For instance, one popular model posits that some students are verbal learners, some are visual, and others are kinesthetic. The matching hypothesis argues that we should use lots of words when teaching verbal learners, lots of pictures when teaching visual learners, and lots of hands-on activities when teaching kinesthetic learners. This makes a lot of intuitive sense, and many educators who have adapted their teaching to reflect the matching hypothesis have had success in improving student learning. These are the educators who give me angry looks when I say that learning styles don't exist.

The thing is, they don't.

And by that, I mean that the matching hypothesis isn't supported by research. Harold Pashler and colleagues conducted a meta-analysis of research on learning styles in 2008, and they reached two conclusions: 1) There aren't a lot of rigorously designed educational studies that test the matching hypothesis, and 2) those that have been conducted provide evidence *against* the hypothesis.[1] Since then, additional studies have continued to refute the matching hypothesis.[2] As some have pointed out, it's true that students have preferences for how they learn, but it's not true that matching instructional methods to those preferences helps student learn better.[3] A lot of educators have seen this research and are tired of educational "experts" touting the value of learning styles. They're the ones who cheer when I say that learning styles don't exist.

Linda Nilson, author of *Teaching at Its Best*, acknowledges this research and argues that educators should move away from talking about learning styles and toward talking about teaching modalities.[4] In her chapter on learning styles, she makes two points about teaching modalities, both well supported by research. The first is that different content benefits from different modalities. For example, most students learn biology better through pictures than words, and most students learn poetry better through words than pictures. The second point is that people learn better when multiple modalities are used. That is, most students learn biology or poetry better through words *and* pictures than either modality alone.

PRINCIPLE 5. *When students work with new material using different kinds of media, they are better able to learn that material.*

Here's my story about multiple modalities.[5] During my senior year of college, I studied abroad in England and Ireland through a program at my university. While we were in Ireland, we focused on the troubled political history of that country in the twentieth century. The textbook on this topic we read before traveling was informative but incredibly dry. Watching the 1996 Liam Neeson movie *Michael Collins*, a biopic about one of the leaders of the 1916 Easter Rising in Ireland, helped provide a narrative for one thread of the topic. Actually visiting the locations described in the textbook and dramatized in the movie made the stories and information more concrete for me, and hearing from various Irish experts while we were there helped me connect the history we had studied to the current political state of the country. Any one of these modalities would have been insufficient for me to get a handle on the twentieth-century history of Ireland (particularly that textbook!), but their combination was incredibly effective.

People learn better when multiple modalities are used. I believe this explains the apparent effectiveness and continuing popularity of learning styles. An educator who adopts the matching hypothesis starts looking for multiple instructional modalities to build into their teaching. They'll find a way to handle a topic through words and pictures and activities in an effort to reach students who are (hypothetically) verbal, visual, and kinesthetic learners. But then they'll teach a class using all of those modalities, which benefits all the students in the room, regardless of learning preference. It appears that the matching hypothesis is working, when in fact it is the use of multiple modalities that is leading to greater student success.

Why does using multiple teaching modalities help learning? One reason is what's known as *dual coding*.[6] We have both verbal and visual channels in our brains that we use to process information. When we encounter a new idea or concept through both words and pictures, we tap into both of these channels, and when the channels are working together, they help us understand and remember that idea or concept. Consider the NASA Goddard Space Flight Center satellite photo (fig. 19), which shows the confluence of the Paraná and Paraguay rivers in South America during flood stage. The two rivers have different sediment patterns, including color and density. As a result, when the rivers come together, they don't fully mix. Instead, they create a new sediment pattern that has elements of the individual streams. In a similar way, when our brains take in verbal and visual information, those streams are combined into something new that unites individual input. That's dual coding.

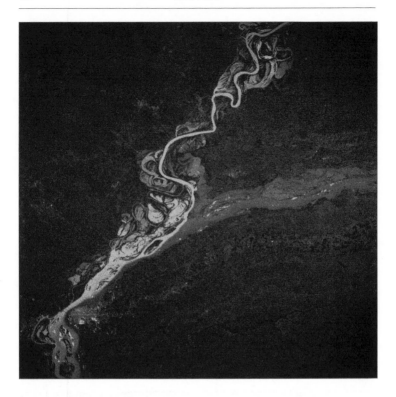

Figure 19. Satellite image of the confluence of the Paraná and Paraguay Rivers. Image by NASA.

Notice that I've gone a little meta here by using a visual metaphor to describe the concept of dual coding. In doing so, I've illustrated one way we can leverage dual coding in our teaching: sharing visuals that complement the verbal descriptions of ideas and concepts we want our students to learn.

This is, sadly, not how PowerPoint is typically used. We've all suffered through "Death by PowerPoint," when a presenter stuffs as many words on a slide as they can, then reads them aloud as their presentation. One might be tempted to think that PowerPoint slides leverage dual coding since processing a presentation like this involves using both eyes and ears. However, our brains use the same verbal channel to process both the words we hear and the words we see. Death by PowerPoint overloads this verbal channel by asking the audience to listen and read at the same time, resulting in neither working very well. When I'm in a presentation like this now, knowing what I know about dual coding, I just look down and listen. I get more out of the presentation when I look at my shoes!

There is a better way to use PowerPoint and other presentation software. When making a point, find an image that represents that point visually, either concretely or metaphorically. Then share that image on screen as you speak. A well-chosen image will complement your verbal delivery instead of competing with it. Your audience will get to use their verbal and visual pathways together, and they'll be in a better position to understand and remember what you want to tell them. If you've never experienced a presentation that practices the principle of dual coding like this, go read Garr Reynolds's book *Presentation Zen*.[7] You'll never look at a PowerPoint presentation the same way.

This chapter isn't about making better PowerPoint presentations, however. It's about giving students assignments that go beyond the traditional five-page paper. There's nothing wrong with a five-page paper; students need practice writing. But if we want to engage students in multiple modalities, we should consider assignments that include more than just the written word. Digital technologies make it easy (well, easier) for students to create artifacts that include pictures and images, videos and sounds. Multimodal assignments that are aligned with our teaching goals give us an avenue to use technology to foster deeper student learning through dual coding.

Note that most of the examples in this chapter come from my home institution, Vanderbilt University. That's not because Vanderbilt has the best multimodal assignments around. It's because my teaching center has been exploring a "Students as Producers" approach to course design for several years now.[8] Students in these courses are encouraged to tackle open-ended problems, to operate with a significant degree of autonomy, and to share their work with wider audiences. "Students as Producers" is shorthand for an approach to teaching that helps students become not just consumers of information but also producers of knowledge, engaging in meaningful, generative work in the courses they take. This work often takes a multimedia form, which makes the "Students as Producers" approach useful for thinking about multimodal assignments. But first, an example from outside Vanderbilt of a faculty member engaging her students as producers through a multimodal assignment.

From Critic to Creator

Tia Smith teaches mass communication at Xavier University of Louisiana. Xavier is the only historically black and also Catholic institution of higher education in the United States, which gives it something of a unique teaching mission. "A lot of my assignments involve creating spaces that are more humane," Smith told me.[9] Her courses often explore the intersection of media and social justice. One of her favorite assignments involves an exploration of hashtag activism, the use of social media to raise awareness about issues of interest. "I know it brings awareness," Smith said, "but then what? Is awareness going to change policy?" To help her students answer these questions, she asks them to create digital ethnographies of their favorite online activists, following and engaging the activist on Twitter or Instagram or their social media platform of choice.

The hashtag activism assignment engages students as critical consumers of media, but Smith isn't satisfied to have students only analyze how media works. To help her students understand how media is created, she asks them to become producers. One of her assignments challenged students to take photos around New Orleans, where Xavier is located, that show how millennials think about feminism. Another required her students to write and record poems about the social justice issues they discussed in her class. For these assignments, Smith determined the medium for the student work, but for others, she let students have an open field. They find that challenging, but Smith wants her students to gain experience with open-ended assignments. "If I'm giving you an open field, where do you go? Where do you run?"

For a course on women in media, Smith put together an assignment inspired by the recent passing of actress Della Reese. She asked her students to use whatever media they liked to make an argument about women in media through a fictitious superhero named Della. "At first, the students were intimidated by the space of options," Smith said, "but then they got into it." One group created a photo essay about Della, focusing on her embodiment as a superhero through close-up images of hands and feet. Another group put together a short film about Della and how she fought crime around campus with her long hair. And a third group produced a radio call-in talk show about Della, one that involved discussions of feminism, representation, and the #MeToo movement. The student groups were interdisciplinary, and they were able to bring their various lenses to imagine ways to use media and technology to explore feminism and superheroes. Smith graded the projects on their use of theories and concepts from the class, the students' use of research to support their work, and the creativity they brought to their medium of choice.

By asking her students to shift into the role of creators, Smith is helping her students not only to be more thoughtful media producers—something important for the mass communication majors in her class—but also to be more critical consumers of media. When her students take the time to consider how they frame an object in a photo essay, they're more prepared to analyze the design choices they see in the visual media they encounter. "When you begin to understand the choice and agency" behind the production of media, Smith said, "and how a story is put together with technology, you become more considerate of it." By putting together arguments about, say, feminism and superheroes through sound or images or video, her students are challenged to think more deeply about those arguments, how they might convey those arguments, and how others make arguments through multimedia. This gets to the heart of Smith's learning objectives for her students.

Smith's assignments require students to use digital tools to create media, but access to those tools can be a challenge for her students, who sometimes struggle to pay for books and fees, let alone smartphones and video cameras. Even Smith's mass communication majors who are planning careers where digital tools will be important struggle with access. "It's a matter of shame for students to come forward,"

Smith said, "and say, 'Look, I want to be a professional, but I don't have the tools.' " They want to be successful, but they need a little help. Smith will assign group projects, structuring the groups so that each has at least one student with a smartphone. She'll also stay late to work with students whose only access to technology is the campus computer lab. But she'll also direct students to more affordable technologies and help them plan ways to save up to purchase those technologies over time.

Smith doesn't shy away from talking about access and shame with her students. She knows she can't assume they all have the tools they need, but she also knows that she can help her students move into the professional work they see in their futures. And she uses multimodal assignments to help her students think more critically about their approach to that work.

Thinking Outside the Boxplot

The interplay between students as media consumers and media creators can play out in a variety of teaching contexts. In 2012 I was teaching a statistics course for engineering students for the fourth time. In an effort to make the course a little more interesting for me and more relevant for my students, I added an emphasis on data visualization to the course.[10] I found that the data visualization material in most of the statistics textbooks on the market looked like it was from the 1950s, with stem-and-leaf plots and box-and-whisker plots and other old-school visualization tools. Modern data visualization tools, including heatmaps, treemaps, and bubble charts, are far more sophisticated and increasingly important in a world where very large, multidimensional data sets were readily available. I knew that students could use these tools not only to find and share stories within complex data sets but also to understand the structure of those data sets and how that structure reflected the statistical concepts they were learning in my course.

Teaching my students modern data visualization tools meant connecting my students with material beyond the textbook. Early in the semester I showed them one of Hans Rosling's well-known TED

Talks, one in which he used an animated bubble chart to tell a story about family size and life expectancy in the developing world over time.[11] After we discussed the visualization tools Rosling used in his talk, I gave my students a complex data set of their own to visualize, one that included carbon footprint and biocapacity information for individual countries. I asked my students to sketch possible ways to visualize some of the data using pen and paper. See figures 20 and 21 for some of the better submissions, modeled on Rosling's bubble chart approach.

I was particularly impressed with the sketch in figure 20, as those students realized the importance of the line $y = x$. Countries below this line, like the United States, produce more carbon than they can store; countries above this line, like forest-rich Finland, have excess carbon storage capacity. During class, I was able to show several student sketches on the classroom projector, which provided the opportunity to discuss strengths and weaknesses of the visualization schemes my students proposed.

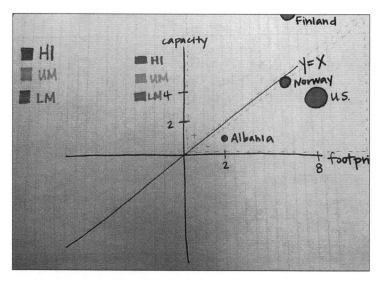

Figure 20. Student data visualization sketch from a 2012 statistics course.

Students continued to practice their data visualization skills throughout the semester, thanks to biweekly problem sets, all of which included targeted visualization questions, and to a few social bookmarking assignments like the ones I used in my cryptography seminar. (See chapter 3 for an introduction to social bookmarking.) One assignment asked students to find and bookmark an example of data visualization, the more complex the better. Students found a variety of examples, many of them what would be considered *infographics*—aesthetically pleasing images designed to communicate quantitative information and to be shared easily online. Topics ranged from fast food consumption to basketball player quality to aboveground woody biomass (that is, where the trees are). As a follow-up to this assignment, I asked students to select a data visualization bookmarked by a classmate and leave a comment responding to the

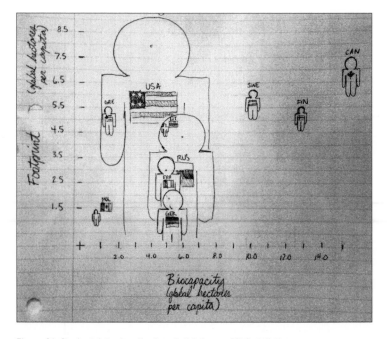

Figure 21. Student data visualization sketch from a 2012 statistics course.

prompt, "What questions about the data does this visualization lead you to ask?" This assignment generated a number of interesting questions, and I got useful insight into the ways my students analyzed data visualizations they encountered.

These opportunities for practice and feedback led to the final project in the course. I asked my students to apply the statistics techniques they learned in the course (primarily hypothesis testing and linear regression) to answer questions about a real data set and to communicate their findings through an infographic. I had given students a version of this assignment in past offerings of the course, but instead of the infographic I had asked students to produce a five-page paper conveying their findings. Although that was a useful assignment (my students will surely need to write technical reports in their future careers), I knew that if my students had to communicate their work through infographics, which feature both text and visuals, they would be in a better position to tell the stories they found in their data sets and to understand those stories and their statistical significance.

The results were, in general, impressive. Figures 22 and 23 picture some of the infographics my students created from both the 2012 and 2016 offerings of the course. I found that my students didn't need much technical help creating their infographics beyond some in-class instruction on producing graphs in R, an open-source statistical tool we used in the course. Students put their infographics together using a variety of free and commercial tools, then submitted their work as images or PDFs.

The infographic in figure 22 is typical of a trend in the 2016 offering of the course: lots of projects about baseball. There's a recent tradition of applying statistics to baseball (sabermetrics, as it's known, as seen in the movie *Moneyball*), of course, but, well, I'm not a sports guy. I never would have selected baseball as a context for a statistics project, but many of my students did. One of the advantages of offering a more open-ended project like the infographic assignment is that students can take the project in a direction they find interesting. The infographic in figure 23 also illustrates this, since the students behind this infographic leveraged some of the geographic information

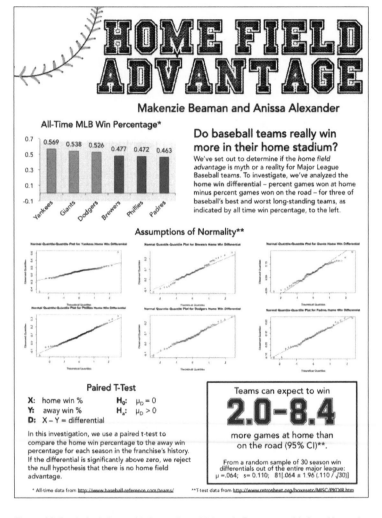

Figure 22. Statistics infographic by students Makenzie Beaman and Anissa Alexander.

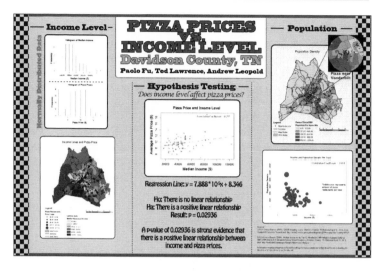

Figure 23. Statistics infographic by students Paolo Fu, Ted Lawrence, and Andrew Leopold.

systems skills they had learned in an engineering course they were taking concurrently.

Another advantage of giving a multimodal assignment like this one is that students are more interested in sharing their work and seeing their classmates' work. I scheduled a seated poster session for the last day of class. Given the stadium seating in the classroom, I asked students to bring printed copies of their infographics to pass around the room while they remained seated. Students spent the hour looking at their peers' work and voting on the best infographics in three categories: Most Interesting Application, Most Sophisticated Statistics, and Best Visualization. It was a fun way to wrap up the semester and it gave students a chance to apply their new skills in data visualization as they shifted back from creator to consumer.

Mass communication and statistics are fields that lend themselves to more visual assignments, but let's now consider how multimodal assignments can work in a discipline that has a much stronger verbal tradition.

Show and Tell in Literature Courses

Something is in the water in the Vanderbilt English department.

I keep running into English instructors on my campus doing really interesting things in their classes. I described the one-time "blog-father" of the English department, Humberto Garcia, in chapter 2, and I'll share how senior lecturer Elizabeth Meadows uses a digital timeline to turn her class into a learning community in chapter 6. In this chapter, however, I share stories from three instructors at very different stages of their careers, all teaching literature at Vanderbilt, all using multimodal assignments for very specific purposes.

Haerin Shin is currently as assistant professor of English at Vanderbilt, and she teaches courses in science fiction, Asian American literature, and new media. Given that range of topics, Shin tends to see students from a range of academic backgrounds, from computer science to film studies, and she encourages her students to use those varied perspectives to explore course questions and themes. She also wants her students to have experiences in her courses that they can use in their future careers, which only occasionally include graduate studies in literature. To that end, Shin offers her students a choice for their final projects: they can complete and submit a traditional research paper, or they can produce a creative project of their choice. Her students have gone in a variety of directions for these creative assignments, sometimes leveraging skills from their previous academic experiences, other times pushing themselves to learn in new ways.

For instance, a political science major in Shin's science fiction course, Jung Min Shin (no relation), built a website that explores the boundary between the real and the unreal through the story of *The Velveteen Rabbit*.[12] The site uses words and images from the children's book, along with examples from other texts from the course, to make an argument about the ways technology is changing the boundary between the real and the unreal (figs. 24 and 25). The argument is a nonlinear one, with the viewer following links embedded in the site pages to navigate through the site along paths they choose, inspired by Shelley Jackson's work of hypertext fiction, *Patchwork Girl*. The student had never built a website before but wanted to learn how to do

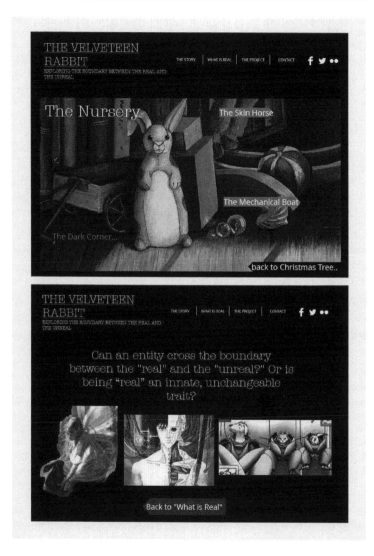

Figure 24 (*top*). Screenshot of Velveteen Rabbit website by student Jung Min Shin, nursery page.

Figure 25 (*bottom*). Screenshot of Velveteen Rabbit website by student Jung Min Shin, real/unreal page.

so in order to better understand the way technology shapes narrative and story in our digitally enhanced culture.

A science major with prior computer programming experience in that same course took a different approach. Miguel Moravec planned his final presentation in the course, required as part of the academic "conferences" Shin organizes during the last week of classes, as a conversation between himself and an artificial intelligence (AI) in the process of gaining self-awareness. He created a short digital video ahead of time, one that portrays the AI side of the conversation, then played that video during his presentation, as he acted out the human side of the conversation (fig. 26). To be clear, Moravec didn't design an AI, he created a short film about an AI! His conversation with the pretend AI during his presentation became a kind of performance piece exploring notions of identity and humanity and how artificial intelligence might go horribly wrong.

Other students have adapted the classic board game Life to explore privilege and power in the United States, created autobiographical webcomics capturing experiences at the intersection of race and ethnicity and gender, and designed digital art mashing up the seven deadly sins and stereotypes of Asians and Asian Americans. Projects aren't required to be digital—the Life remix was decidedly analog—but they are required to make an argument, either through the projects themselves, as in the case of *The Velveteen Rabbit* website, or in the reflective statements students submit along with their final projects, as in the case of the AI performance piece. In those statements, students share the "reasons why they decided to go with a particular form, content, or idea," Shin told me, along with "how and whether they found [their project] effective."[13] Although Shin's students' projects have a strong creative element, the students are also required to include critical analysis, much like Tia Smith's digital assignments described earlier in the chapter. Students have to work with multiple texts, make arguments, and cite their sources. Instead of doing so in a traditional research paper, the students are given the option to do so through a variety of media, using those media to construct and display their reasoning.

Elsewhere in the Vanderbilt English department, Mark Schoenfield

Figure 26. Screenshot from video of student Miguel Moravec's AI presentation. Video courtesy Haerin Shin.

also uses multimodal projects that reside at the intersection of creative practice and critical analysis. Schoenfield is a full professor of English, and he has been thoughtfully experimenting with his teaching practices for as long as I've known him. Recently, Schoenfield added a digital storytelling assignment to his introduction to literature course. He asked his students to create digital stories, following the pattern for digital stories outlined by StoryCenter, a nonprofit arts organization based in Berkeley, California, previously known as the Center for Digital Storytelling.[14] These digital stories are typically short digital videos, no more than ten minutes in length, featuring spoken word, still images, and a music soundtrack. They usually feature first-person narratives with anecdotes and reflections, all structured to tell a particular story, often a very personal one.[15] Schoenfield saw this multimodal assignment, with its structure and intent and constraints, as a tool to have his students experience creative practice in a way that would inform their critical analysis.

One of Schoenfield's students shared a story from his time working at a sheriff's office, a story about a man whose apartment was shot up and the man's search for justice. Another student related a story from her childhood visits to a small town in Mexico and the girl she befriended there whose life was very different from her own. Two students tackled the subject of climate change in their digital stories, one by combining a poem about birds and flight with news sound bites about weather, and another providing a reflection on global warming through the lens of her experience skiing in Colorado. All of the students had to think intentionally about how they used words and images and sounds to tell their stories in fairly short time frames, usually three to four minutes. Schoenfield wanted this experience as creators to inform the critical work his students did in the course analyzing poems. And it worked, at least in a small way. "Because of the assignment," Schoenfield told me, "students paid more attention to the word choice in the poems we read."

Schoenfield shared that observation during a meeting of the digital storytelling working group that he co-led with Vanderbilt sociologist Laura Carpenter, a working group sponsored by the Vanderbilt Institute for Digital Learning. As I participated in that working group, I learned that digital storytelling assignments seem to work best in a course when the form of the digital story aligns well with course objectives. In Schoenfield's case, the short duration of the digital stories his students produced required them to choose their elements carefully, which informed their analysis of word choice in the poems they studied. In Carpenter's case, she wanted students in her sociology courses to better understand the relationship between individuals and society, so having students produce digital stories in which they connected personal experiences to larger issues made sense. My cryptography seminar considers the role of encryption in today's society, which brings up issues of surveillance and privacy, and I imagined asking my students to create digital stories that explored ways they manage their own digital privacy in order to help them see personal connections to the larger debates we consider in the course. I ended up going in a different direction for a multimodal assignment in my crypto course, but I found it useful to look for alignment between medium and learning objectives.

Kylie Korsnack also teaches in the Vanderbilt English department, as a graduate student instructor. Her writing courses regularly feature opportunities for students to revise their work, but she finds that students sometimes struggle with revisions. "Too often students think about revision as simply editing and proofreading," Korsnack writes. "However, by converting their work from a print to a digital format, students have to truly *re-see* their argument from a different angle."[16] To address this, Korsnack sometimes asks her students to take an essay they wrote earlier in the semester and convert it from text to some other digital format. By requiring students to translate their arguments from one medium (the essay) to some other medium, these *digital revisions* help students see their writing from a fresh perspective, which in turn prepares them to refine their writing practices in future assignments.

One student turned his essay on Mary Shelley's *Frankenstein* into an interactive narrative in the style of a Choose-Your-Own-Adventure book.[17] Every few paragraphs, the reader is presented with a choice of paths forward (fig. 27). Clicking on either option reveals different parts of the continuing narrative. As the reader explores the interactive narrative, they encounter the ideas from the student's original essay. By revising his essay to fit this branching structure, the student "had to really think about the structure of his essay and how the parts connected," Korsnack told me. The digital revision helped this student understand the role that transitions play in writing to connect one idea to the next, a role that Korsnack emphasizes in her writing instruction. The platform the student used to create his interactive narrative, Inkle, isn't open to new users at this time, but I hear that Twine works very well for telling nonlinear stories.[18]

Another student took her essay on leadership in the Hunger Games novel *Mockingjay* and revised it as a Pinterest board. She, too, had to think carefully about the structure of her argument as she translated it to a pinboard in which bookmarks ("pins") to other websites are represented through images and supplemented with brief captions. In her essay, she compared the leadership qualities of two characters from the novel. In her pinboard, each character received one pin for each of the leadership qualities she considered. If she judged the character stronger in that quality, the pin was shown with an image of the character from the movie adaption. If the character was weaker in that quality, she used fan art of the character. This schema made

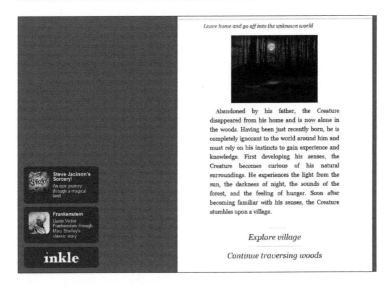

Leave home and go off into the unknown world

Abandoned by his father, the Creature disappeared from his home and is now alone in the woods. Having been just recently born, he is completely ignorant to the world around him and must rely on his instincts to gain experience and knowledge. First developing his senses, the Creature becomes curious of his natural surroundings. He experiences the light from the sun, the darkness of night, the sounds of the forest, and the feeling of hunger. Soon after becoming familiar with his senses, the Creature stumbles upon a village.

Explore village

Continue traversing woods

Steve Jackson's Sorcery!
An epic journey through a magical land

Frankenstein
Guide Victor Frankenstein through Mary Shelley's classic story

inkle

Figure 27. Screenshot of student Zachary Ellington's choose-your-own-adventure website.

the structure of the student's argument visible, to herself and to any viewers of the pinboard.

Perhaps most telling was the student who revised his essay as a Prezi. As we saw in chapter 4 on knowledge organizations, a Prezi can act as a mind map of sorts, laying out spatially the relationships among a set of ideas. When this student shared his Prezi with the class, Korsnack asked him, "Did you learn anything about your writing process by doing this?" His response: "When I mapped my essay out visually, I could see why it wasn't working before." Moving from the verbal medium of text to the visual medium of Prezi helped this student get to the heart of the revision process, seeing his own work differently so he could refine and improve it.

I know how hard it can be for students to practice deep revision of their writing. I see that every semester I teach my writing seminar. It's a first-year writing seminar, and the college has guidelines about how many pages of writing the students in the seminar should produce.

I used to feel constrained by those guidelines, thinking that I could only have my students produce essays and papers in the course. My colleagues in the English department have inspired me, however, to go beyond just text in the assignments I give my students to help them tell stories and construct arguments. I've also been inspired by a colleague in a very different field—health policy—who made a small change in medium in one of his assignments, from the written word to the spoken word, to great effect.

Health Policy Radio

Gilbert Gonzales teaches health policy at Vanderbilt University. A couple of years ago, he participated in one of the course design institutes my teaching center offers, one themed around "Students as Producers." The next semester, his students became producers . . . podcast producers, that is.

One of the goals Gonzales sets for his Introduction to Health Services course is to have students read and understand current research in health policy. Another goal is to provide students opportunities to make a difference in the world outside their classroom. To help meet these goals, Gonzales introduced a podcasting assignment into his course. Gonzales gave his students a list of recent research articles in his field, covering such topics as the effects of healthcare legislation on low-income Americans, the prevalence of Cesarean sections in Mexico, cost-sharing in European healthcare systems, and workforce shortages in Zambia. Students, working individually or in pairs, selected articles from this list to read and then translate for a general audience through ten-to-fifteen-minute podcast episodes. They had to cover a fair amount of ground in their episodes, explaining the research itself—the questions asked, limitations of the studies, the results generated—as well as discussing implications of the research. Students could connect the study to healthcare policy or campaign-trail debates about healthcare. (This course ran in an election year.) Or they could relate the study to healthcare practice and the healthcare decisions of everyday individuals and families.

The model Gonzales used for his students' podcast episodes was the kind of healthcare story one might hear on public radio. These stories share research results and implications for a general audience, in ways that are understandable to someone without specialized healthcare policy expertise. Learning about healthcare is "like learning a new language," Gonzales told me. "You have to learn the differences between an HMO, a PPO, a POS, different types of health insurance."[19] The podcast assignments gave his students a chance to practice that new language. Students were asked to submit full scripts in advance of recording their episodes, which allowed Gonzales to provide feedback and guidance both on the content of the podcast episodes and on the ways students used the language of healthcare. The final products, all of which involved the students' voices to some extent, required students to use that language with fluency, so that their audio stories sounded natural and accessible.

Very few of the students simply read their text into a microphone, however. Gonzales's grading rubric asked students to demonstrate "creative expression," and students took this in different directions. Some used clips of existing audio, some interviewed each other about their research articles or talked to campus experts. Some walked around campus to conduct "person-on-the-street" interviews to include. One team even created fake commercials to break up their podcast episodes. All of these format choices were intended to serve the storytelling needed to make the research understandable and relatable to the intended audience. Crafting that story, in turn, required the students to understand the research they read and its implications. The role of audience was critical here, since students knew their episodes, if approved by Gonzales, would be made public as part of the class podcast, *Healthcare Policy Radio*, available via the audio distribution platform SoundCloud.[20] "I think that really raised the stakes on the quality of the work," Gonzales said, "because they knew that whatever they submitted to me at the end would be available for the world to hear. I think that they responded positively to it." (We'll talk more about the role of authentic audiences in student learning in chapter 7.)

Gonzales said his students didn't need too much assistance making their podcast episodes. He spent one class session going over the assignment and teaching his students to use Audacity, a free, open-source audio editor. After that, they were largely on their own, but few had problems producing their episodes. I had the same experience the next year, when I introduced a podcast assignment into my cryptography seminar inspired by Gonzales's assignment. In my case, I wanted my students to explore the history of cryptography, so each episode considered a different code or cipher, how it works, and why it's interesting. I called my class podcast *One-Time Pod*, a play on the term "one-time pad," a cipher that's used just once and is thus perfectly secure.[21] My students needed a bit more technical help—they probably needed half a class period just before the episodes were due for troubleshooting—but the real challenge was their general unfamiliarity with podcasts. I have a thirty-minute commute to work, so I listen to a lot of podcasts. I forget that not everyone does! Before the assignment, I asked students to listen to a few episodes of my favorite podcasts, *99% Invisible* and *The Memory Palace*, that dealt with cryptography, and we discussed the podcast producers' storytelling choices in class. This helped get my students ready for the assignment, but I still had one student point out that in a three-week span he went from never having even listened to a podcast to producing his own episode.

Gonzales and I aren't the only Vanderbilt faculty teaching with podcasts. Larisa DeSantis teaches in our Earth and environmental science program, and for several years she has asked her students to produce podcasts and other media to communicate the science they were learning. One very talented student, a member of the university's a capella vocal group, made a YouTube video in which he adapted a pop song to explain the change in vegetation that occurred during the Miocene epoch.[22] In the video, he sings all parts of the multipart harmony, and it sounds great. And DeSantis tells me that his science is "100% accurate." Other Vanderbilt faculty have had students produce podcasts in communication studies, sociology, and education.[23] One reason for the popularity of podcast assignments on my campus is that podcasts are having a moment culturally. Another is that the production tools for podcasts are more accessible than ever. A lot of faculty are interested in helping students learn to communicate in a variety of media, beyond the traditional written word found in research papers, and podcasting is a relatively easy first step toward greater digital fluency. When my students share in their producer's statements the intentional choices they made regarding sound effects and background music, I know they're thinking more deeply about the content of their podcasts and practicing a sort of aural dual coding.

Gonzales and I also found that grading podcasts was way more fun than grading papers, which leads me to the most common question I hear from instructors when I share examples of non-traditional assignments like podcasts . . .

Crowdsourced Rubrics

"That sounds great, but how do you grade these things?" That's a good question.

Sometimes, grading isn't that important. For her digital revision assignment, Kylie Korsnack wasn't interested in evaluating the quality of her students' digital projects. She just wanted to know that they had learned something about their own writing process. She kept the stakes low for the assignment, making sure it didn't contribute much to the overall course grade and grading her students largely on completion and the quality of their reflective statements. But for some multimodal assignments, creating a more rigorous grading scheme can be important, both for clarifying your expectations for student work and providing students feedback they can use to improve their understand and skills. This can be particularly true when asking students to create something in an unfamiliar medium or format, like an infographic or a podcast episode. When we ask students to produce something other than the traditional college research paper, they can be unsure how to go about the work and can have trouble connecting their work to overall course goals. In these cases, I recommend a good rubric, and I recommend, when possible, that students have a role in the design of that rubric.

In table 3 is the rubric for the infographic assignment described earlier in this chapter. This type of rubric is known as an *analytic rubric*. It consists of a number of components, along with descriptions of levels of quality within each component and a mapping of this scheme onto a scoring system. There are other types of rubrics, including *holistic rubrics*, which lack component breakdowns but provide synthetic descriptions for each grade an assignment might receive.[24] However, I find that analytic rubrics are generally the most helpful, especially for nontraditional assignments. The rubric seen here went through several iterations before arriving at its current form, and most of those iterations involved input from my students. When I first gave this assignment, they hadn't made infographics before and I hadn't graded infographics before, so I planned a collaborative process to outline and communicate expectations for the assignment.

At the start of class one day, I distributed copies of a few of the infographics the students had found earlier in the course for one of their social bookmarking assignments. I asked the students to discuss the infographics in small groups, sharing what made them work and where they could be improved. Then I shared with the students the rubric I had used to grade the previous version of this statistics assignment, when the product was a five-page paper. Structurally, the rubric looked like the one for the infographic assignment, but the content of the old rubric was different. This gave my students a sense of the kind of rubric I wanted to make for the infographic assignment.

Next I invited the students to a shared Google Doc, a spreadsheet with the same columns as seen in the analytic rubric. I asked the students to return to their groups and identify components of an effective infographic based on their discussion of the sample infographics I had given them. I asked them to add their components to the Google spreadsheet and to draft quality descriptors for their components. If you've never seen dozens of students contribute to the same Google Doc concurrently, you should try it sometime. It's rather exciting. Within minutes the students started populating the Google spreadsheet with new rows, all potential contributions to the rubric I would use to grade their infographics later in the semester.

After class, I took the Google Doc and edited it down into a draft rubric. There was a lot of redundancy in the spreadsheet, with multiple student groups identifying the same or similar components. This made sense given the process we used, and it was a good thing, too,

Component	Poor (1 point)	Acceptable (2 points)	Good (3 points)	Excellent (4 points)	Score
Content					
Questions	There's no central question addressed in the project.	There's a central question addressed in the project, but not explicitly.	There's a central question explicitly addressed in the project.	More than one interesting question is addressed explicitly in the project.	
Methods (Double points for this row!)	The methods used to model the problem and answer the question(s) posed are entirely inappropriate.	The methods used have potential to model the problem and answer the question(s) posed, but are applied in inappropriate ways.	The methods used to model the problem and answer the question(s) posed are (for the most part) appropriately applied.	The methods used to model the problem and answer the question(s) posed are not only appropriate, but show signs of creativity.	
Assumptions	Assumptions (about normality, about the relationship between the sample and the population) are not stated in the project.	Assumptions are stated in the project, although the assumptions are inappropriate or poorly explained.	At least one appropriate and clearly explained assumption is stated in the project.	All appropriate assumptions are clearly explained in the paper.	
Computations	Several obvious computational mistakes	A few obvious computational mistakes	At most, only a couple of obvious computational mistakes	No obvious computational mistakes.	
Answers	Answers to questions raised in the project are provided in the context of the problem without clear connections to the mathematical models used.	Answers to questions raised in the project are provided based on the mathematical models used, but not in the context of the problem itself.	Questions raised in the project are answered in the context of the chosen problem with a connection made to the math models used, but the connection is fuzzy.	All questions raised in the project are clearly answered in the context of the chosen problem.	

Table 3. Analytic rubric for an infographic assignment in a statistics course.

Component	Poor (1 point)	Acceptable (2 points)	Good (3 points)	Excellent (4 points)	Score
Communication					
Organization	There's no obvious structure to the infographic.	There's some structure to the infographic, but it's sloppy or hard to follow.	Infographic is structured well (using headings, arrangement, and whitespace), but there's no conceptual basis for the organizational scheme.	Infographic is structured and spaced well, with a clear conceptual basis for the organizational scheme.	
Spatial Relationships	Spatial relationships (axes, areas, etc.) in the infographic obscure, not convey, meaning.	Some spatial relationships convey meaning, but many have no particular meaning.	Spatial relationships are generally used to convey meaning, with some exceptions.	Spatial relationships are used to convey meaning and show signs of creativity.	
Colors	Colors are chosen arbitrarily or seemingly without reason.	Colors neither distract nor aid in the communication of information.	Colors are used to convey meaning or otherwise enhance communication.	Colors are used to convey meaning and are aesthetically appealing.	
Text	Text is used in the infographic in confusing or arbitrary ways.	Some useful explanatory text is provided, but not much.	Infographic text is used to explain the context of the problem and clarify purposes of visualizations.	Text and visuals work together so that each is enhanced by the other.	
Sources	There's no attempt to explain sources of data or of ideas drawn from outside the course.	Some attempt at sourcing is made, but sources are unclear or ambiguous.	Sources are clearly provided, but it's unclear how they were used.	Sources of data and of ideas drawn from outside the course are clearly provided, as are the ways they were used.	
Aesthetics	Hurts the eyes.	Dull and uninteresting.	Pleasant enough.	Attractive, with notably creative elements.	
Total (out of 48)					

Table 3 (*continued*).

since it pointed to aspects of data visualization where we had a lot of consensus. There were student-contributed components that didn't work for me, and I didn't mind cutting those out. And there were aspects of effective infographics that the students collectively missed, so I added those in. But there were also places where the students did a really good job of describing levels of quality for a given component. That row about aesthetics in the final rubric that includes the phrase "hurts the eyes"? That was a student contribution.

The result was a pretty good infographic grading rubric. I decided we needed to test it, however, so I spent another class session having the students use the draft rubric to grade some more sample infographics. Remember the activity I described in chapter 3 that combined a grading rubric and a classroom response system? That's what this class session looked like, with the classroom response system showing me where the students understood the rubric and where they weren't able to apply it consistently. The activity allowed me to further refine the rubric before using it to grade the students' final infographics and to provide students feedback on their work. For each student infographic and each rubric component, I marked a level of quality, from poor to excellent, and I provided written comments to the students explaining my evaluations, particularly where they missed the mark. The structured nature of the rubric made grading go fairly quickly and it facilitated feedback, but it was the process of constructing the rubric that helped my students better understand my expectations for the assignment, particularly the use of visuals to communicate statistical information, which my students still found challenging even after multiple activities in this area earlier in the semester.

During the class session where the students graded sample infographics using the draft rubric, we spent a lot of time discussing the "spatial relationships" component. What does it mean for spatial relationships to convey meaning? We looked at a vertical axis that didn't start from zero and talked about how that affected our impression of the data. We considered a series of items ordered left to right and wondered why some items were placed to the left of other items. We looked at a graphic showing country flags of various sizes and asked whether the size of the flag was meant to represent the population or the GDP of that country. That is, we looked at the ways quantitative data can be represented visually and how the visual design choices we make affect how data is interpreted. Doing this translation back and forth between numeric and visual helped my students understand how data is structured and how we find and share stories within data, and that's why a multimodal assignment like this one was so useful for this course.

Spending two entire class sessions developing and testing the rubric was a lot of class time, but I felt it was time well spent given how focused it was on key learning objectives for the course, like understanding how spatial relationships convey meaning. The next time I taught the course, I tried to save time by skipping the first phase, where students brainstormed rubric components, but I don't think the infographic assignment was as successful. It's hard to tell, since I had reduced the focus on data visualization elsewhere in the course, too, but I didn't feel that the students demonstrated the same level of understanding about spatial relationships in their final products, and they didn't seem to value data visualization as a learning goal as much as the first group of students did.

That points to one of the benefits of this rubric creation process. Students not only come away with a better understanding of the learning goals for a nontraditional assignment like this one but also often value those goals more. For instance, my statistics students initially thought that infographics were all about aesthetics, about design choices like color or font intended to make the final product more visually appealing. Those are important choices to make while creating infographics, but they didn't seem relevant to a statistics course. Distinguishing between "spatial relationships" and "aesthetics" on the rubric helped my students see why I was giving them such an unusual assignment and what I wanted them to learn from it. I saw similar benefits when I used this process to develop a rubric for my podcasting assignment, and I would expect it to work well for a variety of nontraditional assignments where students might be justifiably wondering what the point is.

One downside of such a structured approach to rubrics is that students might not bring as much creativity to their work if they feel they need to fit it in a given set of boxes. Some instructors chafe at the prescriptive nature of an analytic rubric and prefer to give their students looser guidance on expectations. This can result in creative and outstanding work, but it can also leave some students floundering on their projects. An analytic rubric, especially when complemented with the kind of structured activities I've described here, can produce more consistent, if not as impressive work. This is also an approach that can work well for more traditional assignments, including those five-page papers. Not all our students come to our classrooms knowing what's expected of them even on traditional assignments, and many struggle to complete those assignments. Guiding students through an analytic rubric creation process can create a more inclusive learning environment, particularly for first-generation college students and students who have had less academic preparation for our courses.

Practical Advice

What are some good practices when giving students multimodal assignments beyond the use of rubrics as described above? Consider the following suggestions.

1. Be clear with yourself and your students why the assignment is a useful one for the course you're teaching. Make sure there's an alignment between the format or medium of the assignment and your learning objectives. Mark Schoenfield wanted his students to attend to word choice in the poems they read, so he gave them a digital storytelling assignment that required careful attention to scripting. Gilbert Gonzales wanted his students to be fluent in the language of healthcare, so he gave them an assignment that required them to speak about healthcare into a microphone. If you can't make these kind of connections, consider a different type of project.

2. Replace, don't add. That is, don't feel like you need to add a multimodal assignment to an existing course when it might make more sense to replace a more traditional assignment. Or, like Haerin Shin, give your students the choice between a paper and a project. Be careful not to overload your students, especially if you're not sure how much work the multimodal assignment will take.

3. Give your students a little autonomy, whether that's in choice of topic, format, or style. Autonomy is highly motivating, and students will often use the freedom you give them to connect the project with personal or professional skills or interests. Choices can also help more students find ways that work for them to meaningfully represent their learning.[25] If you give students a very open-ended assignment, however, make sure you have a plan for directing them to your learning goals within that freedom and a plan for evaluating their work. Sometimes a more focused project, like a podcast assignment, is easier to plan for but still allows some student autonomy.

4. Students will need practice with new skills. That includes technical skills, like video or audio editing, but also discipline-specific skills, like graphing a five-dimensional data set or telling a story through sound or following a nonlinear argument through a hypertext document. Build small opportunities for practice and feedback along the way, before the big multimodal assignment.

5. Students will also need feedback on their work in progress. For more open-ended assignments, requiring a project proposal early in the process can help you redirect students who aren't heading in useful directions. For all multimodal projects, requiring a draft or outline or script or storyboard once the project is underway provides an opportunity for guidance and course correction before more intense production begins. Peer review can be helpful here, too, especially if you have a rubric to help structure peer feedback.

6. Ask students to submit a designer's statement. As noted in chapter 3, there are often key decisions that reflect student learning that aren't evident in the final product. Did the student use that smart color scheme on her infographic intentionally? Why did the student cut sixty seconds from his draft digital story? What reasons did the student have for selecting the music they used in their podcast episode? A reflective statement of some sort, one that takes you behind the curtain, so to speak, can be very useful when evaluating student work. And the practice of self-reflection will help develop the students' metacognition.

7. Determine which technological tools you'll learn to use and plan to spend some time teaching your students those tools. Don't feel like you need to be an expert on all possible tools useful for your assignment, but do get comfortable using a core set of tools that any of your students might use. For my infographic assignment, I taught my students to generate particular types of plots using R, the free statistical software we used in the course. For his podcasting assignment, Gilbert Gonzales taught his students to use Audacity, a simple but free audio editing tool. Our students were welcome to use other tools they knew—my students assembled their infographics using everything from Microsoft Paint to Adobe Illustrator, and some of Gonzales's students opted for more feature-rich programs like GarageBand or Adobe Audition—but we made sure we could troubleshoot with students who stuck with the tools we taught them.

8. Make one yourself. We often ask students to do things we don't do ourselves (or haven't done in a long time), but for these nontraditional assignments, it can be helpful if you have some experience creating the product you're asking your students to create. Even if you don't produce, say, a podcast episode from start to finish, having some experience doing the thing can inform your assignment design, increase your

empathy for students who are struggling, and equip you to provide useful feedback to your students as they work.

9. Share! All of the instructors profiled in this chapter used some mechanism to share student work with other students. An end-of-semester poster session or showcase is a great option. I remember the first time I gave my math students an application project. As I was grading, I thought it was a shame that I was the only one to see some of the more interesting projects. The next semester I added a poster session so that the students would have a chance to learn from each other. More on this idea in the next two chapters.

10. Use a rubric. I know, this list was meant to be good practices beyond the rubric. But, seriously, rubrics are great. Look for ways to use them to clarify your expectations, prepare students to do interesting work, and give students actionable feedback on their learning.

CHAPTER 6

Learning Communities

I PLAY a lot of board games. I play with my family. I play with my friends. I've hosted board game nights at the teaching center where I work. I've gone to local board game conventions and played with strangers. I once played a sixty-six-player version of the strategy game Settlers of Catan at a convention in Nashville. It was epic. My personal board game collection is . . . healthy. Last time I counted, I had more than seventy-five games in my game closet, from family games like Sleeping Queens and Love Letter to modern classics like Carcassonne and Dominion to off-beat titles like Tokaido, which features competitive vacationing in seventeenth-century Japan, and Herbaceous, a game all about growing and potting garden herbs. I'm always looking for new games to bring to the table or add to my collection, and I track all of my plays on an app on my phone, so I know which games I've played the most.

All that board game playing requires some work, however. I'm always learning how to play new games, for instance. Most modern board games come with printed instructions or "how to play" videos that explain their rules well, but sometimes I need a little help interpreting a rule here and there. The website BoardGameGeek is invaluable in those instances. Almost every game under the sun has a discussion forum there, and I can be reasonably confident that if

I'm running into a rules question with a particular game, someone else has, too, and has posted something about it on BoardGameGeek. And if no one has, I'll post my question to the game's forum and I can usually get a response within a day or two, sometimes from the game designers themselves.

Once I've learned a game, I'm often called upon to teach it to new players. Sometimes that's because I'm the one who wants to play it, and I find a convenient family member to break in the game. Other times it's because my friends know I'm the guy who teaches teachers, and they know I'll do a pretty good job explaining the game to them. The folks who make those "how to play" videos? They're excellent teachers, too, and I love listening to interviews with them when they talk about their approach to teaching games. They have provided me with a few techniques that I've been able to incorporate into my practice.

I like playing board games because I like the challenge of figuring games out, not just how to play them, but how to play them well. And I like the social component. I spend enough of my time behind a screen; I appreciate sitting around a table with friends and having a good time in person. Board games also feature excellent art and graphic design, and I have found that I enjoy taking and sharing photographs of games. I'm not the only one, either. The board game scene on Instagram is robust, and I've learned a number of approaches to shooting board games from Instagrammers I follow. My friends have gotten used to pausing when a game is over, making sure I have a chance to get a good picture before they put away the pieces.

I share this not because it makes me cool. (I have an advanced degree in mathematics, so I gave up on cool a long time ago.) No, I share this because I've learned a lot about board games—how to play them, how to teach them, how to photograph them—from other people like me who like to play board games. I've never read a textbook on board games, I've never taken a class on board games, and I've never consulted with an expert on board games. There is one podcast I listen to that's cohosted by a professor of game studies, but, for the most part, I learn about board games from the board game community.

This isn't unusual. Lots of people have hobbies they learn about through particular communities. One of my board game buddies is also into woodworking, and he's often sharing plans for projects with other amateur craftspeople online. I have a friend who's a quilter, and she participates in various online quilting discussions and competitions. A librarian colleague learns computer languages in his spare time, sometimes from online courses but often just by swapping code with other practitioners on GitHub. Our students do this, too, whether they're learning to make animated films from YouTubers or diving deep into sports statistics on fantasy football forums or figuring out how to beat a video game from other gamers' playthroughs. One study showed that 86 percent of the posts in a *Worlds of Warcraft* discussion forum involved "social knowledge construction," that is, solving problems through discussion, knowledge sharing, and debate.[1] There's a lot of serious learning that happens in fun spaces. When our students want to learn something new, they often find a relevant community and then learn from and with the people in that community.

Then they walk into a college classroom.

Much of the time, a college classroom is structured physically and organizationally to position the instructor as the sole source of expertise in the room. Stadium seating points all the chairs to the front of the room, where the professor professes. Enrollment management systems list courses as "lecture" courses because that's what's supposed to happen during class, right? Instructors end classes by asking "Any questions?" because they're the ones with the answers. Classes don't have to work this way, however. And, of course, many don't. Many instructors have found ways to help their students see each other as sources of useful experiences, perspectives, and expertise. We can turn our classes into *learning communities*, where our students learn from and with each other.

> **PRINCIPLE 6.** *Structured ways for students to learn from and with each other can enhance the learning experience for all students.*

Consider Margaret Rubega's #birdclass activity, mentioned in chapter 3, where students report bird observations via Twitter. Not only does this activity make visible to her the ways the students are transferring what they learn in class to the world around them, but it also provides a venue for students to share what they're learning with each other. A student can easily search Twitter for "birdclass" or click on the #birdclass hashtag in a tweet to see all the observations posted by their peers. The student observation that the design of a golf course seemed to divide bird territories becomes as valuable, maybe more valuable, than a note in a textbook about the effect of the built environment on bird ecology. And it's one thing to hear about camouflage in a lecture; it's another to see a photo taken by a classmate that morning of a camouflaged killdeer nest just a few miles from campus. Having students submit these observations to the instructor via email or Dropbox would haven't nearly the same utility. The hashtag creates a learning community.

Or consider the social bookmarking activity from my cryptography course using Diigo, also mentioned in chapter 3. Most weeks I give my students a category of resources to bookmark, like cryptography in the news or military cryptography, but within those parameters students often find ways to bring their personal and professional interests to the topic. There's the student planning to be a software developer who shared links to articles on quantum cryptography, a potential revolution in computer encryption. There's the Sherlock Holmes buff who bookmarked articles on cryptography in literature, including the conspiracy theory that author Lewis Carroll was secretly Jack the Ripper. There's the student who started the course seeing Edward Snowden as a hero, whose bookmarks explored the intersection of surveillance and privacy. And there's the student majoring in Russian who always managed to find a Russian connection to share, no matter what the bookmarking assignment was. My students brought such diverse interests to the course, and our Diigo assignments provided a platform for them to share those interests so we could all benefit.

That's an important point about learning communities. Instructors are members, too. When we create structures that invite and encourage our students to share their interests, experiences, and opinions, we open the door to learning from our students. We don't have to lose our role as authorities and experts, but by asking our students to contribute to our courses in intentional ways, we show them that learning is an ongoing process. And we can find our own teaching energized by what our students share.

It's important to note that students aren't likely to participate as enthusiastically in a course-based learning community as they would in a community built around one of their hobbies or interests. Motivation, particularly intrinsic motivation, is a key factor here. Students taking a required introductory statistics course just aren't going to jump into discussion forums or Twitter chats like those playing fantasy football or comparing theories about *Stranger Things*. However, there are multiple aspects of motivation. Self-determination theory proposes three primary needs that motivate behavior: autonomy, competence, and relatedness.[2] Learning community activities like #birdclass and social bookmarking tap into all three to varying levels. By allowing students some freedom to choose what they tweet or bookmark, we help meet their need for autonomy. By giving students assignments like these that aren't too challenging and by praising students who share really interesting finds, we help them feel competent. And, perhaps most importantly, by having students share what they're learning with each other, we help them feel connected to the course community and thus help meet their need for relatedness.

The rest of the chapter features stories from other classrooms where instructors have used technology to tap into these motivations and to help students learn from each other. One note on terminology first, however. The term *learning community* has been used in a variety of ways in the educational literature. Sometimes it refers to the practice of linking two courses, so that the same students take both courses and benefit from connections between the two curricula, and sometimes it refers to living-learning communities, where curricular work is combined with residential campus experiences.[3] Those are educational practices that have proven to be effective, and some of the technologies mentioned in this chapter can play useful roles in those kinds of learning communities. That said, I'm using the term in a different sense, closer to how it is used by the Center for the Integration of Research, Teaching, and Learning. Learning communities are courses or other learning experiences where there is shared discovery and learning, functional relationships among learners, connections made to related learning and life experiences, and where the learning environment is inclusive.[4]

I'll say more about creating inclusive learning environments later in the chapter, but for now let's consider some ways that educators have used technology to turn their courses into learning communities.

Course Blogs in Astronomy

"There's so much stuff in astronomy—it's the entire universe—and we only have a semester to talk about it."

Erika Grundstrom loves astronomy. She is the director of astronomy labs at Vanderbilt University, and she teaches astronomy to students from kindergarten to college. She hosts regular stargazing parties on top of a campus parking garage, to which she invites students and friends. She has a portable planetarium she takes to area schools. She was fully prepared to drive up to eight hours to find cloud-free skies for the 2018 full solar eclipse if the weather in Nashville was poor. Her son's middle name is Cosmo.

Erika Grundstrom loves astronomy.

Her quote above is in reference to a course on solar system astronomy she teaches at Vanderbilt, a course that enrolls between forty and fifty students, mostly nonscience majors, each spring. The course covers a variety of topics, including naked-eye observation, light and telescopes, terrestrial worlds and planet formation, and life in the solar system. But there's so much more astronomy that Grundstrom—and her students—find exciting. Looking for a way to leverage that excitement, Grundstrom set up a course blog back in 2012 and asked her students to blog about astronomy regularly during the semester. At the time of this writing, she has seven years of student posts on her course blog.[5] What began as an effort to help students experience a universe of ideas has turned into a vibrant learning community.

Grundstrom asks each student to create a WordPress blog, and she asks students to post multiple times during the semester. The first post is an introduction, where students share their interests in the course and practice embedding images and including hyperlinks to other websites. After that, students are required to post twice for each of the units in the course. One post needs to be directly about one of the topics in the unit, while "the other one could be about anything they could convince me was astronomically related," said Grundstrom.[6] Students share their personal connections to astronomy, examples of astronomy in the news, and whatever else they find as they follow internet rabbit holes related to astronomy. Since WordPress handles multimedia well, students often embed entertaining videos or animated GIFs, giving their posts a little character.

Grundstrom created a course blog that uses a tool called FeedWordPress to aggregate posts from the student blogs. All of her students' posts with designated categories or tags are automatically copied to the course blog, and when a visitor clicks on the duplicated student post, they are taken to the student's individual blog, where the visitor can comment and read other posts by that student. This course blog setup, which is sometimes called a *motherblog*, means that all of the student blog posts are easily found in a central location that is searchable by date, category, and tag, but comments and discussion happen on the students' own blogs.[7] It also means that students get to personalize their blogging space, selecting from a variety of WordPress themes and templates. And since students control their own blogs, they are free to blog about topics other than astronomy or continue blogging after the course concludes.

Students are also asked to comment on their peer's blog posts each time there's a blog assignment, and this is where the course blog really shines. Grundstrom found that students need some guidance on commenting. Initially, too many comments were of the form "That was a great blog post!" which didn't generate the kind of conversation Grundstrom wanted. She now provides her students advice on commenting, recommending that good comments "refer to specific details in the post and then add to the conversation," perhaps by asking a follow-up question or linking to another blog post or relevant resource. She provides comment templates, such as the following.

- You made some good points here, such as _____ . I agree with them because _____ .
- I disagree with the point you made about _____ . The reason I disagree is _____ .
- A point about this you may want to think about is _____ . The reason you may want to think about it is because _____ .

Students generally follow Grundstrom's commenting advice, and the resulting conversations are often engaging, particularly for students who posted ahead of the assignment deadline, since those posts attract more comments. For instance, several students posted about the discovery of gravitational waves in February 2016, a discovery that confirmed the existence of something theorized by Albert Einstein almost a century earlier. This was big news in the astrophysics community, and Grundstrom's students noticed. One student titled her post "Gravitational Waves!!!!" (with four exclamation points) and included an accessible summary of the discovery.[8] Another student commented on that post, noting with some wonder how old the technology was that the scientists used in their experiment, which led to a back-and-forth with the original poster about the value of investing in resources for astronomy and astrophysics. A third student commented, linking to his post on the same news, and a fourth student added to the discussion about the history behind gravitational wave research.

That same semester, another student blogged about the gravitational waves discovery but used the news to share a reflection on how humans make sense of gravity.[9] "Is it fun bouncy times with color, like in the new OK Go video? Is it a destructive thing of despair like in the Clooney/Bullock blockbuster? Is it a higher dimension hitherto inaccessible to us humans in our current plane of existence but manifests as the power of love in a tesseract?" (The second and third questions are references to the movies *Gravity* and *Interstellar*, respectively.) This post generated several comments from peers, including an observation that gravity is often seen in a negative light and a suggestion for improving the visual metaphors used to understand gravity. One commenter pushed back, writing, "Sounds like you might have synesthesia instead of actually thinking about physics. Science is thankfully very different than literature and arts in that it is concrete. This all sounds very fishy and more like a literary assignment rather than a science post." The original poster, however, had a strong response:

> I would respectfully disagree. As a physics major in my senior year, I have had plenty of time to ponder the concreteness of the scientific method, but that wasn't the point of the post. I am a creative writing major also, and wanted to gauge how non-science majors think about concepts in physics, namely gravity. I understand the inherent differences in human endeavor when it comes to understanding a scientific concept vs a literary one, and that was largely the point of this post. Thanks for your input.[10]

Grundstrom uses blogs to create an environment where students are encouraged to make personal connections to course material and to learn from the connections their peers make. This can lead to disagreements and the occasional testy comment, but Grundstrom and her students find the blogging assignments useful and engaging. The commenting requirement is key here, since it means students are motivated to actually read each other's posts and to comprehend those posts well enough to form a response that moves the conversation forward. And the public, persistent nature of the course blog means that each new cohort of students joins a larger learning community stretching back multiple years. In spite of the thousands of posts on Grundstrom's course blog, I suspect she and her students won't run out of astronomy topics to discuss anytime soon.

Video Killed the Discussion Board Star

A course blog can be an excellent way to have students share ideas and perspectives. Blogging is a text-based medium, however, and some instructors have found more success with student-produced videos as a means to create learning communities.

Enoch Hale is the director of the Center for Teaching at Learning at Humboldt State University. He teaches courses on pedagogy and leads faculty development seminars on a variety of topics. One of the seminars he taught while at Virginia Commonwealth University focused on the design of learning spaces—how the furniture, technology, and configuration of a classroom can promote good teaching and learning. Hale set up a motherblog for the seminar participants using WordPress, asking each to create their own individual blog to share reflections as they progressed through the seminar. However, Hale found that the conversations on the blogs weren't as rich as the face-to-face conversations the faculty had when they met in person, so he asked the participants to move their online discussion to a platform called Flipgrid.

Flipgrid is an online discussion board, but it's entirely video-based. An instructor creates a "grid," a bulletin board of sorts for their class. Each item on the grid consists of a prompt from the instructor along with a series of student responses. All the responses and, optionally, the instructor prompt are videos recorded using a laptop webcam or a smartphone camera. The platform is mobile friendly and doesn't require logins for students, so it's easy to use. Since students can respond using their phones, they'll sometimes shoot their videos on location. (One student filmed from his backyard next to a fire pit, and he used fire as a metaphor in his response.) The videos are short, with the typical ninety-second limit meant to encourage concision as well as informality. Before participants add their own video responses, they have the option of viewing previously submitted responses. Since those responses are all brief, this isn't a big ask of participants.

Hale leveraged that feature in his work with the seminar on learning spaces. Instead of asking participants to post a response to his Flipgrid prompt, he would ask them to watch the most recent participant video and respond to that instead. For instance, during a week in which he asked faculty participants to have their students rearrange the furniture in their classrooms, his prompt was "What insight did your students come to as a result of shifting their furniture?" The first respondent on Flipgrid was to answer that question and pose a question for the second respondent. The second respondent answered that new question and posed their own question. This continued down the line, creating a chain of participant responses, each no more than ninety seconds of video. This structure required participants to listen to and learn from each other.

"People actually want to hear what others have to say," Hale told me.[11] The purpose of Flipgrid is to capture individual reflections, "but I also want to use it to encourage greater discussion," discussions that build on and inform in-person discussions. Hale's prompts can go in a lot of directions, especially for his pedagogy courses. "Identify two assumptions made by the author in this argument and their implications for broader discourse" after a reading, or "Complete this statement: I used to think . . . but now I think . . ." as an end-of-semester prompt. These are open-ended prompts, where there is value in seeing the different directions students go in their responses. This means there's value in viewing a peer's Flipgrid contribution.

Kris Shaffer also asked his students to create ninety-second videos designed to benefit their peers. While teaching an online music cognition course at the University of Colorado at Boulder, Shaffer put together an assignment that leveraged the theory of dual coding, helped students build out their internal knowledge organizations, and strengthened his learning community by having students produce a collaborative course resource. The final product was a concept map built in Prezi focused on core concepts for the course—pitch, tonality, meter, syntax, interference, chunking, habituation, and more. Each concept was represented by a short video created by a student, and the relationships listed on the map between concepts were also developed by students.

Shaffer used a multistep process to create this collaborative concept map. First, students were asked to create short explanatory videos of important course concepts. Each video had to explain the concept in the student's own words and include an example from a piece of music that illustrated the concept. Students were encouraged to discuss their videos-in-progress on Slack, which Shaffer used as a discussion board for the class, but the final videos had to be their own work. Students produced two videos per week for three weeks, with some opportunity for revision. Next, as the videos came in, students were asked to submit written explanations for the relationships between pairs of concepts represented in the video. For instance, a student might select the concepts echoic memory and pitch, and provide an explanation for the connection between those two ideas. Students were asked to submit three explanations per week.

Finally, Shaffer selected the best student video for each concept and the best student explanation for each pair of concepts and assembled them into a concept map in Prezi. The resulting map covered the breadth of the course and served as a resource for students as they worked on their final, open-ended project. The map was useful at that point of the course, but the process used to develop the map was also useful along the way. Students had to view their peers' videos in order to complete the relationship assignment each week. "Students are implicitly making mental notes as they look at each other's work," said Shaffer. "They're always evaluating their own work against it, and plugging that into their future work." They would "steal" ideas from each other from week to week, effectively saying "Oh, that worked really well, so I'll do that next week on this other concept," Shaffer added. This led to better and better student contributions during the course, as students learned not only concepts from each other but ways to explain those concepts concisely and effectively.

Both Hale and Shaffer were very intentional in their use of technology to foster student interaction. Hale asked questions on Flipgrid that benefited from multiple perspectives, and Shaffer used an iterative process in which students could learn from each other's contribution from week to week. When giving assignments aimed at building learning communities, it's important to structure them so that there is genuine value to student learning when students view and respond to each other's work. The next story also features an instructor thinking intentionally about students learning from each

other and another multimodal class resource constructed collaboratively by the students themselves.

Love, Marriage, and Timelines

In chapter 4 on knowledge organizations, I mentioned Bryan Lowe's
use of the digital timeline platform Tiki-Toki to help his students
think about the religions of Japan both across time and within a time
period. Lowe isn't the only one of my Vanderbilt colleagues to use
digital timelines in this way. Elizabeth Meadows teaches in English
and women's and gender studies, and she put Tiki-Toki to use in her
course on love and marriage. However, where Lowe's students each
made their own timeline, Meadows asked her students to create a
collaborative class timeline.[12]

The course focused on the "shifting meanings and cultural functions" of love and marriage in Great Britain and the United States
from 1500 to the present. Meadows asked her students to document
some of those meanings and functions on a shared class timeline on
Tiki-Toki. Students provided a variety of contributions that served
as commentaries on marriage and its changing meaning over five
hundred years, from quotes from Jane Austin's *Pride and Prejudice*
to an analysis of an 1879 Texas law on the management of marital
property to 1921 census data showing a significant population gap
between men and women in Great Britain.

As in Bryan Lowe's class, students were asked to cite their sources
and were encouraged to include multimedia resources and links to
additional information where possible. Students also slotted each
of their contributions in one of three categories: legal, literary or artistic, and religious representations of love and marriage. Timeline
contributions were made throughout the course, and students were
graded along the way, which allowed for changes in practice when
they had trouble—like the time several students placed a text on
the timeline according to its publication date in an anthology, not its
original publication date.

Meadows, like Lowe, also asked her students to write a final paper
using the timeline as a resource. But where Lowe's students used their

individual timelines, Meadows students drew upon the class timeline, which by this point in the semester had hundreds of entries. This was 2014, a year which saw a number of legal rulings in the United States regarding same-sex marriage, so Meadows asked her students to concur with or dissent from a recent judicial ruling using elements from the timeline. This turned the timeline from an exercise in visual bibliography into a class resource that all students could draw from. It can be rare for students to cite their own work from earlier in the semester, but seeing students cite each other's work on their final papers? That's really exciting. Meadows found the papers enjoyable to read, and her students were proud of the online resource they had produced.

There are a number of digital timeline tools that allow collaboration, and I've used a couple in my own teaching. For instance, I've asked my cryptography students to contribute to a shared class timeline on the history of cryptography, then write a paper in which they explore lessons learned about keeping or breaking secrets from the examples in the timeline. That assignment used a tool called TimelineJS, which integrated well with timeline data entered in a Google spreadsheet. Tiki-Toki, however, seems particularly easy to use, especially with students. Another Vanderbilt colleague, Keith Weghorst, recently taught a course on democratization for the political science department. He asked his students to document developments in democracy around the world through a number of shared Tiki-Toki timelines.[13] Each student was given a different country, and student contributions were rolled up together in four timelines, each covering a different region of the world. Each country received its own color, making it easy for students to compare developments in democracy across a region. As in the other examples, Weghorst asked his students to draw on their class timelines for their final projects.

That seems key to the effective use of a resource created collaboratively by students—asking them to do something with the resource, either along the way or once it's finished. I didn't do that the first time I used a collaborative timeline in my cryptography course, and the timeline contributions felt a bit like busywork. The "lessons learned" paper fixed that problem, though I still had to push my students to analyze examples of cryptography outside those described in our textbook.[14] Social bookmarking can also create a useful shared resource, particularly if you direct students to bookmark resources likely to be useful in later papers and assignments. It really does feel great when I see a student citing some other's students contribution to our shared Diigo group!

Open Textbooks and Social Reading

Some instructors have their students create a class resource. Robin DeRosa has her students actually make their own textbooks.

DeRosa teaches at Plymouth State University, a small, rural, public university in New Hampshire. She realized that the eighty-five-dollar anthology she required for her early American literature course consisted almost entirely of works in the public domain. In the interest of saving her students money, she wondered if she could assemble a comparable anthology out of copies of these texts that were free of copyright. Over the summer, she worked with a team of research assistants (that she paid out of her own pocket) to locate such copies, starting with texts she knew she wanted to cover in her course. By the fall she had them loaded into a draft textbook on Pressbooks, a platform built on WordPress that provides a number of tools for publishing books.

The students that fall were both surprised and grateful to have a free textbook. However, it wasn't a fully featured anthology like the ones DeRosa had used in the past. It lacked the kind of introductory and supplemental material that provide students with historical and biographical context for the texts they were to read. So DeRosa had students write it themselves! Students drafted, revised, and edited introductions to all the major texts (including one rather entertaining sixty-second video recap of a Thomas Paine work[15]), as well as maps, glossaries, discussion questions, and assignments. Some of the texts in the anthology lacked modernized spelling, so students engaged in some light editorial work, too. Their work can be seen in the current version of the textbook, *The Open Anthology of Earlier American Literature*.[16]

Can students write the kind of textbook content that's usually authored by experts in a field? "I contend," DeRosa told me, "that there's nobody better equipped to explain foundational disciplinary knowledge to an undergraduate than another undergraduate." She mentioned an example of students explaining the Haitian revolution to each other in the ancillary materials they created for their open anthology. "I've been teaching for twenty years, and I thought, you're doing this way better than I did, because you totally get what students don't get. It's really hard for me with my PhD to understand what you don't get."

Although the building blocks of DeRosa's first student-made textbook were works in the public domain, she argues that having students write textbooks can work in areas outside of literature. She has followed a similar process to develop open-source, student-created textbooks in two other courses at Plymouth State, an introduction to interdisciplinary studies and a first-year seminar. "The disciplinary knowledge in any commercial textbook is not proprietary. Nobody owns the foundations of physics." Just as Kris Shaffer had his students explain key concepts in music cognition to each other through short videos, students in a variety of disciplines can create textbook materials. If putting together an entire textbook seems like a reach, DeRosa recommends having students enhance existing open educational resources, such as the openly licensed textbooks from OpenStax.[17] Student can rewrite or supplement sections that they find hard to understand or develop examples or problems relevant to local contexts or professional interests.

Not only has DeRosa had her students create open textbooks, but she has also moved into what I like to call the "killer app" of digital textbooks: social reading. She knew that it would defeat the cost-saving rationale of creating an open textbook if students spent their printing budget creating hard copies of the anthology they created just so they could take notes on the readings. So she invited students to annotate their textbook using a tool called Hypothesis. Hypothesis provides a social annotation layer to any website, allowing visitors to highlight and comment on content within the site and to read and

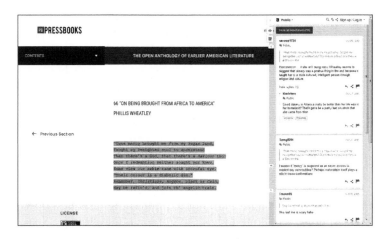

Figure 28. Screenshot of social reading via Hypothesis in Robin DeRosa's literature course.

engage with comments left by other visitors. DeRosa's students used Hypothesis to collaboratively annotate their textbook, discussing the readings together right there in the margin of the digital book (fig. 28). Where student highlights and annotations in print textbooks are private, Hypothesis allowed reading and annotating to become a social activity. The eighteen students in DeRosa's early American literature course added more than *ten thousand* annotations to the open anthology by the end of the semester. I often hear from faculty that students don't do the reading; that wasn't the case in DeRosa's course!

DeRosa had to teach her students how to annotate well. She shared with them different moves one can make when annotating with a group, from pointing out key passages to offering an analysis to responding to an analysis to asking a question to finding a relevant external resource. All of these moves, she tells students, are helpful to the learning community. So is humor, and her students are often quite funny. (She mentioned to me that a few students went on a riff about a Sigmund Freud reading that was hysterical.) She finds that social reading in particular helps students who don't typically enjoy reading. They might not leave as many annotations as their peers, but reading their peers' commentary on the reading helps them understand and engage with the reading. What about assessing her students' annotations? "I love grading," DeRosa said, "because I don't. I just read and respond."

"Textbooks have become community spaces for my courses," DeRosa told me. "Lots of stuff is happening in those textbooks. There's content, but also process, discussion, epiphanies, and community building." And continuity across time, as new cohorts of students engage with the content and annotations their predecessors contributed. "I'm trying to build collaborators, rather than solitary researchers," DeRosa said. "Especially for interdisciplinarians, it's necessary to build bridges between knowledge domains, and doing that collaboratively is more effective." DeRosa also points out that it took time and intentional effort to teach students how to use Pressbooks and Hypothesis and other collaborative tools in her course.[18] Students didn't walk into her classroom knowing how to use these tools or the ethical questions they raise about annotating the work of others.[19] But DeRosa knows that teaching students how to use technology to learn with their peers will serve them well in their future academic and professional lives.

Teaching in Stereo

If you're of a certain age, you might remember View-Master. It was a plastic toy you held in front of your eyes, like binoculars. Mine was red; my mom's was gray. The toy came with circular cardboard reels, each embedded with fourteen tiny film transparencies in seven pairs. The images in each pair were of the same scene, but from slightly different perspectives. When you inserted a reel into the viewing device, you viewed a pair of images simultaneously, one with each eye, creating the illusion of depth in the image you saw, thanks to how vision works with our two side-by-side eyeballs. View-Masters were originally used to share stereoscopic images of tourist attractions around the world, but I recall that I used mine mostly for 3D stills from television shows like *Batman* and *He-Man and the Masters of the Universe*.

In more recent years, the field of photogrammetry has pushed the idea of stereoscopic images to the extreme. It's now possible with consumer-grade cameras to take hundreds or thousands of photos of an object from all different directions, and then stitch those photos together using specialized software (and a fair amount of computing power) to create a highly detailed, three-dimensional, virtual model of that object. Video game designers use photogrammetry to create more realistic game environments, and museums use the technique to share virtual copies of fragile artifacts for researchers near and far to study. One photo provides a flat image of an object. Two photos, taken from slightly different angles, can create the illusion of depth. A hundred photos, taken from many angles, can recreate an object in a virtual world.

When we turn our classes into learning communities, where students are invited and encouraged to share their perspectives on course content, we create the possibility for a kind of teaching in stereo, where all involved learn more deeply as they integrate and synthesize the perspectives shared. When I stand in a lecture hall, throw out a question to a hundred students, and ask for volunteers to answer it, I might hear from several students if I'm patient enough. Research indicates that five to eight students will account for 75 to 95 percent of college classroom discussion, regardless of class size.[20] Most of the students will stay silent. More critically, the students I hear from are often of a certain type. In one class, it might be that I just hear from white students; in another, it's just the math majors. The students who speak up often don't represent the full range of experiences or perspectives in the room. By just taking volunteers to respond to my questions, I'm missing an opportunity to teach in stereo. However, when I make an effort to surface all my students' voices and experiences and ideas, the learning community is in a better position to understand the question at hand more deeply and to think critically about it.

There are a lot of very powerful reasons why students don't speak up in class or contribute their thoughts on a discussion board or jump into using a social reading tool. In the STEM fields (science, technology, engineering, mathematics), women and students of color often hold back in class and indeed change to other majors, not because they don't have the ability to do well in class, but because of classroom climate, lack of role models, curricula in which they don't see themselves, and instructional approaches that deprecate active learning.[21] In all fields, stereotype threat results in students performing more poorly when they are reminded of negative stereotypes they face, from the notion that women are bad at math, or black students aren't ready for college, or white men aren't as good at sports as black men.[22] The implicit, and sometimes very explicit, biases present in every classroom further inhibit student participation in the learning process.

Some of the forces that lead to exclusion in our classrooms are beyond our control. But there are steps, however small they may seem, we can take to create inclusive learning environments, where all students feel more welcome and able to contribute to the learning community.[23] Start by working to build rapport with your students. Learn their names, find ways to invite them to office hours, and provide constructive feedback on their work that sets clear standards while affirming that students can meet those standards.[24] Create a classroom climate that fosters participation. Use inclusive language, make sure your examples and illustrations connect with diverse students, and set ground rules for discussion and debate—ideally by having students help shape those rules.

A comprehensive approach to inclusive teaching is beyond the scope of this book, but there are some specific ways that technology can help us teach in stereo. Classroom response systems, for instance, can allow all students to respond to a question or prompt before they see their peers' responses. Inviting independent answers like this can help surface points of view that might not get shared if some student responses are privileged by being shared first. A variety of social media tools, including Twitter and social bookmarking services, allow participants to use pseudonyms. The anonymity that this provides can make it safer for some students to take a risk by sharing an opinion or resource that's unexpected. Platforms that allow students to personalize how they represent themselves, like blogging platforms with a variety of themes and templates, can help students feel more ownership in the learning process and be more confident in sharing their perspectives. And a variety of technologies, as we have seen throughout this book, can make student learning visible, which is critical to teaching in stereo.

Inviting students to contribute their perspectives comes with some risks, of course. Mechanisms that make it easier for a minority student to share an opinion with the class also enable uninformed and offensive perspectives to be shared. That's why establishing consensus around ground rules is important, as is thoughtful handling of critical incidents. As educator Maha Bali writes, "The more vulnerable we are online, the more imperative it is for us to be able to control our online existence [and] presence on our own terms, not anyone else's."[25] Explore the literature and talk with colleagues about inclusive teaching practices as you find ways to use technology to give your students a greater voice in their own learning experiences.

Practical Advice

Much of the practical advice from earlier chapters applies to using technology to foster learning communities. Consider also the following steps aimed at creating environments where students learn from and with each other.

1. Ask open-ended questions. Provide prompts and assignments that benefit from multiple perspectives, ideas, or examples so that there's room for lots of student contributions. Sometimes having students work toward a single best answer is useful, perhaps through a wiki of some sort, but even then, look for problems that allow multiple solution approaches.

2. Encourage students to make connections between course content and their personal and professional interests. This provides students motivation, helps them see the relevance of what they're learning, and, perhaps most important to the creation of a learning community, allows them to bring more of themselves to the collaborative learning process.

3. If students are contributing to the learning community online, be sure to bring those contributions into the classroom. That is, find ways to integrate student contributions in face-to-face conversations and discussions. You might share a few interesting examples yourself, have students share their work or lead class discussions when their contributions are most relevant, or build in-class activities around student contributions.

4. Be okay to say, "Wow, I didn't know that." In an authentic learning community, the instructor learns from the students, too. Sometimes we instructors feel like we have to be the expert on everything or lose face with our students. However, when our students see that we're open to learning new things alongside them, they feel empowered and engaged.

5. When using online platforms to create learning communities, ask students to select recognizable usernames and use avatars or other visual representations that help everyone track who said what. It's not helpful to read an insightful comment in a Google Doc, only to find out it was contributed by Anonymous Aardvark. Names and avatars, even if they aren't real names and photos, help connect contributions to people.

6. Provide structures for peer feedback. For students to learn from each other, they need to consider the contributions made by their peers. This might involve a commenting policy, like Erika Grundstrom's course blog, or a series of assignments that build over time, like Kris Shaffer's collaborative concept map. And note that students might need some instructions on how to provide each other feedback in constructive ways.

7. Grade lightly. As noted in the chapter on formative assessment, light grading involves grading more on effort than quality and keeping the stakes low.[26] Participating in a learning community involves taking some risks, and risk-taking can be inhibited when grading becomes too worrisome. Consider having students assess their own contributions to the learning community at a few points during the course. I've found this kind of self-assessment a valuable tool for helping

students see how their online activity for a course contributes to their peers' learning.

8. Build community across time. A number of the examples in this chapter involved resources that were open to multiple cohorts of students. Imagine several years of students contributing to a shared digital timeline, each year having students add entries and refine existing entries. That's how learning communities often work in non-academic settings; they don't reset every time there's a new semester.

9. If you have students work together on some collaborative resource, like a timeline or concept map, find something useful for them to do with it, preferably something that requires them to make use of the entire resource, not just their own contributions to it. You might ask each student to focus their contributions to a particular category, then assign a project that requires students to look across categories. Or vice versa, having students contribute all kinds of things, then look for themes or groupings within the class contributions.

10. Be ready to teach students to share in productive ways. I had to guide my cryptography students to the kinds of credible resources that would be most useful for their projects. Erika Grundstrom had to show her students the kinds of moves they can make when leaving a blog comment. Plan to make some course corrections with students as you see what they contribute, so that the community gets better at learning together.

CHAPTER 7

Authentic Audiences

IT WAS 2010, the first time teaching my cryptography seminar and my first time teaching writing. I had read that having students read each other's writing could improve their work.[1] The theory is that when students try to explain something to their instructor, they might leave some gaps, knowing the instructor—an expert in the field—can fill those gaps. But when students write for their peers, they work harder to explain themselves, since they know their readers don't have any greater expertise in the field than they do.

I wanted to leverage this effect, so I asked my students to read and comment on three of their peers' papers for the second big assignment in the course. This assignment, which later turned into the podcast assignment I mentioned in chapter 5, was a bit of expository writing. Students had to select a code or cipher from history and write about its origin, use, influence, and mechanics. I needed a way for students to read each other's work, so I posted their papers on the course blog. This was my first time using a course blog, and I wasn't asking students to post there. It was just a space for me to share announcements and resources. However, by posting my students' papers there, the students could easily read those papers and leave comments. And they left quality comments, using some prompts I supplied to craft thoughtful responses to their colleagues' papers. I considered the activity a success, since the students' writing was sharp and their responses were attentive.

Then two things happened that I wasn't expecting.

A few days after the assignment was complete, one of my students came into class and said, "Dr. Bruff, I was Googling my paper topic last night, and my paper is the third result!" I pulled up Google on the classroom computer, and, sure enough, there was Sam's paper, right behind a couple of webpages from the United Kingdom's National Archives. This was back before Google started personalizing search results, so these were the universal Google results for "Great Paris Cipher." Sam said with some disbelief, "Some high school student is going to cite my paper!" I told him, yes, they would, which is great because it was a solid paper. To be fair, there's not much online about the Great Paris Cipher, so Sam didn't have a lot of competition. But it was still exciting to see his work right there on Google.

The next class session brought an even bigger surprise. Another student walked into class and said, "Dr. Bruff, the dude from my footnotes read my paper!" Tanner had written about the Chaocipher, a cipher with an unfortunately goofy name that had a bit of mystery to it for most of the twentieth century. Two fellow students had read Tanner's paper and left comments on the blog, each raising questions about the cipher that Tanner hadn't been able to answer in his essay. Moshe Rubin, an independent cryptography researcher whose website Tanner had cited, somehow found the post, likely through a Google alert on the name of the cipher he studied, and left a generous nine-hundred-word comment answering the questions Tanner's peers had raised in their comments.

That semester was my first experience connecting my students with an audience for their work beyond the classroom. Although I had only put my students' papers on the course blog as a way to help them see each other's writing, in doing so I made their work available on the open Web. As a result, both Google's robots and "the dude from my footnotes" found my students' work and responded to it in their own ways, and my students found that attention rewarding. However, that attention came after my students submitted their work. I wondered if I could build an audience for my students' writing ahead of time, so that the audience effect I had observed would motivate my students while they were still working on their assignments.

The next time I taught the course, I partnered with Holly Tucker, a professor of French at Vanderbilt University who, at the time, edited a group blog called *Wonders and Marvels*. The blog featured daily explorations of the history of science and medicine contributed by a small network of journalists and academics. Tucker loved the idea of having the students in my cryptography seminar write for her blog, just as some of her students had done in the past. She spent an hour with my students that fall talking with them about the *Wonders and Marvels* audience—mostly people with college degrees with a healthy interest in history but no particular backgrounds in science or math—and the kind of writing that interested them. This provided my students with a fairly concrete audience for their expository writing, which was useful in crafting good hooks and deciding how to pitch the more technical aspects of their writing (explaining encryption and decryption systems for their chosen ciphers).

Students submitted their papers to me first for feedback, then revised their papers for a grade from me. I passed the revised papers on to Tucker, who provided students with additional feedback in her capacity as editor of *Wonders and Marvels*. Students weren't required to revise their work a second time based on Tucker's notes, but those who did were then published on *Wonders and Marvels*, where their essays on historical ciphers reached an audience of thousands. Just over half of my students made it to publication, but all of the students benefited from having a clear audience in mind and the potential to have their work appear in front of that audience. Tucker and I felt that the partnership was successful enough that we did it again two years later when I taught the course again, this second time in conjunction with the release of the Alan Turing biopic *The Imitation Game*. Seventeen of my students have work available on her website, including a new piece on the Great Paris Cipher that is the number three Google result for that search term as of this writing.[2] (Sorry, Sam, but you're in ninth place now.)

One more unexpected result came from helping my students make their work public. A few months after the first batch of student essays were published on *Wonders and Marvels*, an editor from the website io9 reached out to Tucker. The site publishes pieces on science, technology, science fiction, and pop culture, and the editor wanted to republish one of my students' essays. Tucker passed the request along to me, and I looped in the student, and we all agreed that it would be fine for io9 to reprint his work. In March 2013, an essay by first-year student Alberto Perez on the World War II Japanese encryption machine known as Purple went up on io9, and it has been viewed by more than ninety-one thousand people at the time of this writing.[3] I knew that having my students write for Holly Tucker's blog would connect them with an audience beyond the classroom, but I had no idea their work would receive an audience so large!

> **PRINCIPLE 7.** *Connecting students to authentic audiences for their work can motivate students toward deeper learning.*

At first by accident, then intentionally in partnership with a colleague, I had practiced in my writing seminar what Bass and Elmendorf call *social pedagogies*. These are "design approaches for teaching and learning that engage students with what we might call an 'authentic audience' (other than the teacher), where the representation of knowledge for an audience is absolutely central to the construction of knowledge in a course."[4] These pedagogies have both cognitive and affective elements. As students work to find ways to convey their understanding of a topic to a particular audience, they must necessarily deepen their understanding of that topic. That's the cognitive piece, and it's what lies behind the adage "to teach is to learn twice." The affective piece is the motivational effect of producing something for a real audience, someone who isn't consuming the work because they have to grade it. The result is often higher quality work and deeper learning for the student.

The "Students as Producers" approach to course design we've been exploring at Vanderbilt leverages the power of social pedagogies, as do the examples in this chapter. Social pedagogies don't require digital technology. For example, Reacting to the Past is a curriculum featuring structured in-person games in which students role-play historical figures through debates and discussion, building their understanding of history as they express that understanding to each other through the game.[5] But if you're looking for something useful to do with technology, connecting students to authentic audiences for their work can be powerful, and technology is pretty good at that. Sometimes making student work public leads to serendipitous success, like "the dude from my footnotes" and my student's io9 publication, but just putting student work on the Web doesn't necessarily mean anyone outside of your class will see it. The following examples feature intentional choices by instructors to use technology to take advantage of the audience effect and to practice social pedagogies.

Science Communication

"What can a student say meaningfully in a four-minute video?"

This question was asked of Chris Willmott by a colleague skeptical of the digital video assignment Willmott uses in his bioethics course. The course is part of the medical biochemistry program at the University of Leicester in the UK. The assignment asks Willmott's students—future researchers and doctors—to create short videos explaining developments in biomedicine and their ethical and social implications. Willmott wants his students to understand the science behind the kind of biomedical research they see in the news and to appreciate the diversity of ethical perspectives regarding such research. Topics have ranged from organ trading to performance-enhancing drugs to donor conception to genetic testing. Willmott's students work in teams over six weeks to create the videos, and Willmott posts the best of the videos on his YouTube channel, BioethicsBytes, where some student-created videos have received more than eight thousand views (fig. 29).[6]

Students have created videos in the style of television news programs, public-service announcements, and short documentaries. They've used roleplays, person-on-the-street interviews, interviews with academics and other experts, handcrafted stop-motion animation, computer animation using tools like VideoScribe, and, in one case, finger puppets. Willmott spends a couple of class sessions preparing students for the assignment, one session on ethics in bio-medicine and another on video production. As part of that second session, he shows examples of similar videos online and has students discuss what was effective or not about those examples, and he shows examples of past student work. Willmott gives his students a few warnings: Comedy is hard. Person-on-the-street interviews usually aren't interesting. And don't use your real name if you're role-playing a doctor accused of medical malpractice. (That happened once, and it caused problems when the student went on to practice medicine!) All the student videos are presented in a showcase at the end of the module, with snacks and a people's choice award, and Willmott posts the best videos to YouTube (after checking for copyright violations) as a carrot for students to produce good work.

What can students say meaningfully in a four-minute video? "An awful lot," Willmott told me. "To make a good four-minute video, they've got to have a fairly rounded understanding of the topic. They've got to understand the material, and then they've got to think about the narrative that they're going to use to take the viewer through it." Willmott tells his students to create videos for a target audience member, "someone with a reasonable grasp of the fundamentals of biology, but not an expert."[7] Willmott doesn't guarantee his students an audience, as I did with my *Wonders and Marvels* assignment. Some of his students' videos rack up thousands of views on YouTube, others just a couple of hundred. And, of course, only the best of the videos are even posted online; the rest aren't seen outside of the classroom at all. That's okay, however, because it's the hypothetical audience that matters for shaping his students' explanations and storytelling.

One of my Vanderbilt colleagues, Ole Molvig, also has his students practice science communication for a hypothetical audience. Where Willmott's students pitch public service announcements at a high-school-educated audience, Molvig's students create children's picture books exploring the notion of revolution in the history of science. One student wrote about the role of mathematics in science through a story about a tree whose fruit turned red, with the red representing the spread of math within science. Another student designed a book about sharing, specifically the sharing of multiple

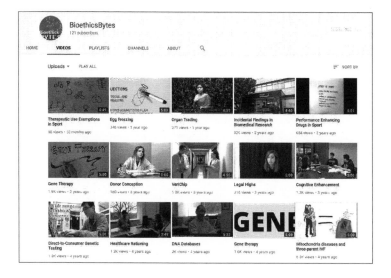

Figure 29. Screenshot of Chris Willmott's "Bioethics Bytes" YouTube channel.

meanings and approaches to science. Molvig's students didn't produce physical books to give to actual children, but the task of distilling a complex topic into a narrative that was interesting and accessible to a school-aged child helped Molvig's students both clarify and convey what they learned in his course.

The audience effect can be stronger when there's an actual audience, but connecting students to real audiences isn't always practical, nor would it be advisable if students aren't ready to have their work seen publicly. In those cases, a hypothetical audience can still provide a lot of structure to an assignment and tap into the cognitive benefits of social pedagogies.

Course Exchanges

As an instructor in Vanderbilt's cinema and media arts program, Jonathan Rattner has always had students share their film projects with each other for purposes of feedback and critique. That's a standard practice in the visual and performing arts. What's less standard is having students share their work with students they don't know at a college five hundred miles away. But that's exactly what he did.

A few years ago, Rattner and a colleague from graduate school, Bridget Draxler, got an idea. He was teaching a course on documentary film history, production, and theory at Vanderbilt. She was teaching a writing course in the English department at Monmouth College in Illinois. His students were producing short, experimental documentary films. Her students were encountering and critiquing various kinds of media. Rattner and Draxler decided to create a *course exchange* through a shared course blog. Rattner's students selected their works-in-progress to share on the blog, and Draxler's students viewed and responded to the films in writing through the blog's commenting tools. This pairing provided Rattner's students an authentic audience for their work, and it gave Draxler's students the opportunity to critique films in conversation with the filmmakers.

"My students were nervous," Rattner told me. "But it took their work to a slightly more serious level." He pointed to the importance of novice filmmakers sharing their work with an external audience. "It helps to break that imagined barrier that we all have that our creative work will be immediately disliked by people who don't know us." Rattner pointed out one student whose first film generated several thoughtful critiques from Draxler's students. The film, a mediation on the purpose of college through the metaphor of wandering, worked as a "forum for dialogue and audience reflection," which Rattner marked as a success. Moreover, the feedback and support from Draxler's students gave the young filmmaker "the confidence to continue to push himself creatively and academically," according to Rattner.

Building community across the two cohorts of students went slowly. That was fine, however, since Rattner wanted his students to share their work with strangers. As the students interacted on the course blog, however, they started to develop some connections, which were solidified when the two classes came together via Skype at one point during the semester. English students aren't often able to ask questions of the authors and creators they study, but that was possible in this case, and the conversations across the two classes helped each group of students understand creative processes a little better, those used by filmmakers and those used by writers. The students were, of course, novices in their respective disciplines, which meant the collaboration had some limitations. Rattner said that he would like to pair one of his courses with another art class, perhaps, "so the critique would be even more rigorous."

The course exchange experiment was successful enough that both Draxler and Rattner have explored similar pairings in subsequent courses. For instance, Draxler and Matt Lavin of Saint Lawrence University were both teaching Martin Luther King Jr.'s "Letter from Birmingham Jail" as part of separate first-year seminars focused on "ways of knowing in the digital age."[8] They loaded a copy of the text on CommentPress, a WordPress tool that allows social reading and annotation, like Hypothesis, mentioned in chapter 6. What followed was a multistep process: students in both classes annotated the text on paper independently, then collaboratively on CommentPress. Then the students discussed the social reading experience together via Skype, then each class on their own. Both groups of students had lively conversations about the "surrealness" of reading together with strangers online, connecting the experience to previous course texts about digital reading and writing.

Meanwhile, Rattner added an assignment to the cinema and media arts senior capstone seminar he teaches. In addition to giving talks about their work, designing professional websites, and completing short festival-ready projects, Rattner's seniors also create educational blog posts for students in Rattner's introductory courses. The seniors are asked to focus on some aspect of the major—production, theory, or analysis—that they find exciting and over which they feel some level of mastery. The blog posts must include some written component, as well as a multimedia component the seniors create, either from scratch or by remixing their own past work. Students have selected such topics as women in film, the long take, the artistic merit of music videos, and film editing tutorials for specific software.

Other instructors, such as Humberto Garcia and Erika Grundstrom, mentioned earlier in the book, have current students read and respond to blog posts written by past students. That provides an interesting experience for the current students, but the posts were generally authored by students who didn't know their work would be read by future students. In Rattner's case, he asks his current students to prepare materials to be used by future students, which leverages the audience effect more directly for those current students. And exchanges between concurrent courses, like the one Draxler and Lavin built around "Letter from Birmingham Jail," take this idea even further.

Having students within a course share and respond to each other's work can turn a course into a learning community, as we saw in the previous chapter. Broadening that learning community to include students in another course, perhaps at an another institution, can be a practical, engaging, and low-risk way to have students represent their learning for an authentic audience. Finding a fellow instructor to collaborate with might take some matchmaking, but given all the courses in all the disciplines happening at any given moment around the world, the possibilities are open-ended.

Hypothetical audiences, course exchanges . . . how else might you connect your students with an authentic audience? Well, you could ask your students to write for the fifth most popular website in the world.

Writing for Wikipedia

A lot of people don't know how Wikipedia works.

Sure, they understand that Wikipedia is an online encyclopedia that anyone can edit. But most people don't edit Wikipedia, and they don't really understand how the sausage is made. Tim Foster discovered a particular, common misconception about Wikipedia while teaching an introduction to Spanish language course at Vanderbilt University. One day in class, a student asked him how to say "Ice Bucket Challenge" in Spanish. Remember the Ice Bucket Challenge? When there were all those videos on Facebook of people pouring ice on themselves? (No, I didn't understand it, either.) When asked about Ice Bucket Challenge, Foster did what he usually did when uncertain about expressing something that specific in Spanish: he loaded up the Wikipedia page for the term and clicked over to the Spanish version.

The student asked, "Is that a good translation?"

Foster replied, "That's not a translation."

Foster quickly realized that most of his students mistakenly believed the language-specific versions of Wikipedia, like the Spanish-language Wikipedia, were simply translations of the English version of Wikipedia. "In that moment," Foster later recounted, "it dawned on me that for the student, they had assumed that all cultural production was in English and that everything not in English was a translation."[9] That's not how Wikipedia works, however. Each language-specific version of Wikipedia is authored by speakers of that language. Some may translate from other language-specific versions of Wikipedia, but, in general, language-specific content on Wikipedia is authored independently. (Visit the English-language Wikipedia page for "Ice Bucket Challenge," then switch to the Spanish-language page. Even if you don't speak Spanish, you'll quickly see that the two pages have different content.)

Later, while teaching an introduction to Portuguese language course, Foster decided to give his students a language production task for an authentic audience, while simultaneously dispelling for his students this particular misconception about Wikipedia. He showed his students the Portuguese Wikipedia page for Nashville, the adopted home of his Vanderbilt students. There wasn't much there, much less than the English language version of the page. He told his students they were going to build out the page to better represent Nashville to Portuguese speakers around the world. This meant brainstorming potential topics, researching those topics, and then writing Wikipedia content in the target language of Portuguese. They spent a week on this class assignment, with each student tackling a different topic, all practicing their Portuguese composition skills.

The final class session in this activity also brought a teachable, if somewhat humbling moment for Foster. He had added a few headers to the Nashville page without also adding content for those sections. During class, as his students were working, he received an email from a Portuguese language Wikipedia editor, one of the thousands of volunteers who help keep Wikipedia up to standards. Wikipedia has a "no stubs" policy, which meant Foster had erred in his editing by posting headers without content, and the editor made this very clear in his email to Foster. Foster replied, right there in front of his students on the big screen, with an apology, then re-edited the Nashville page following proper protocol. The entire interchange was in Portuguese, of course, so students had some reading comprehension practice in addition to a lesson about how Wikipedia works!

Although Foster didn't have his students write for a specific audience, like a writing course at another institution or an established blog, his students were keenly aware that they were writing for a very real potential audience. They knew how often Wikipedia showed up at the top of search results in English, and Foster assured them it was the same in Portuguese. Their representation of Nashville would be read by Portuguese speakers around the world. Indeed, that's the case today, since most of the Portuguese Wikipedia page for Nashville still consists of work by Foster's students.[10] (Look for user Peregrinotim in the version history to see specific contributions by Foster's students. They wrote the content, but he made the page edits.) The audience effect was a powerful one, particularly for the students who went above and beyond Foster's assignment by adding charts and graphs about Nashville weather and other topics. "I don't think I would have seen that extra effort had this been something that just got turned in to me," Foster said. "I think students want their work to be impactful."

Foster is hardly the only instructor to have students write for Wikipedia. I know half a dozen instructors at my institution alone, and there are hundreds more across the globe. Where once college instructors banned students from citing Wikipedia, now the nonprofit Wiki Education Foundation works with instructors to help more than seven thousand students a semester contribute to Wikipedia, according to board member and Vanderbilt anthropology professor Carwil Bjork-James.[11] Many of those students are helping to fill gaps in Wikipedia's coverage. Bjork-James, for instance, teaches a course on human rights of indigenous peoples, and he gives his students a structured Wikipedia assignment that parallels an argumentative essay on the same topic. Writing an encyclopedia article that requires a neutral point of view helps the students separate their opinions about particular controversies from more objective facts. And knowing that they are contributing missing or underrepresented topics to an encyclopedia read by millions motivates the students to take the work seriously.

Making those contributions isn't always easy, since Wikipedia's "neutral point of view" and notability policies, among others, often create the kind of gaps in coverage that Bjork-James wants to fill.[12] However, given how many people rely on Wikipedia to begin (and sometimes end) their research, having students write for Wikipedia means a few more people will know its limitations and how it actually works.

Professional Audiences

"They're not going to be able to get jobs unless they can show what they can do."

Jeff South teaches journalism at Virginia Commonwealth University in Richmond, Virginia. With the state capitol just ten minutes away, South and his colleagues run a program for their majors called Capital News Service.[13] Junior and senior journalism students cover politics and other topics out of Richmond, writing stories that are picked up by newspapers around Virginia and beyond, thanks to a partnership with the Associated Press. The program, based on similar programs at the University of Maryland and elsewhere, has been at VCU since 1994, back when students wrote news articles on typewriters and mailed their articles to newspapers across the state. As with other examples in this chapter, the prospect of an authentic audience means students up their game. "When students realize their story will go across the world," South said, "it's a big motivator. It's beyond grades. They suddenly realize that they have to come through." When they commit to covering a story, "if five o'clock rolls around and they don't have that story, there are going to be news organizations wondering where it is."

Writing for a very real and very public audience comes with some risks. Students make mistakes and, even though each piece is reviewed by at least two instructors, some of those mistakes make it to print. South had a student cover a committee meeting at the capitol, and the student misattributed a quote to the wrong committee member.

Capital News Service had to issue a correction, which was hard on the student. "These negative things are learning opportunities for the student," South told me. "The student who did that will look at attribution in a new way. Once you've made that mistake that the person sitting at the table was senator so-and-so, and it wasn't, that student won't make that mistake again." It's better for students to have that experience as students, not in their first jobs. South noted that news organizations don't provide on-the-job training like they used to. Students need to hit the ground running.

Getting those jobs is another matter. Grades and journalism degrees don't matter as much as they used to with a tightening job market. "The pedigree is less important," South said, "than the demonstration that you can write, that you have experience, that you can go to what would appear to be a very boring city council meeting and come back with a story." South has to connect his students with authentic audiences for their work. If not, he can't provide them the training they need to get and succeed at jobs as journalists. Having those audiences not only helps the students shape their stories and motivates them toward excellence, but it also provides them with a valuable professionalization opportunity. All professions have some role for communication, and professional education can provide similar opportunities for students to practice communicating with authentic audiences.

Doing so can take some hustle, of course. South works hard to find publishing platforms for his students' work. He described a touching story about organ donation written by a nonmajor in a course on science journalism he cotaught with another instructor. The student wanted to know where donated organs and tissue went and who benefited from the donations. He centered his story on a mother who lost a child and had those same questions. South found the story so compelling he pitched it to a former student who ran a local news website, where the story was picked up and published. South knew that there would be many people who learned something from the student's story, and he did what he could to get it in front of as wide an audience as possible.

South uses similar tactics on a smaller scale in his introductory mass communication course, which enrolls a mix of majors and non-majors. The course is taught entirely online, with a mix of lecture videos, Google Hangouts with guest speakers, online small group discussion, and more. One assignment asks students to participate in new media, to better understand the ways technology is changing mass media. South asks his students to complete one of the following activities: create a short video about a banned book and share it on the American Library Association website during Banned Books Week, record and archive an interview with a family member for the Library of Congress using the StoryCorps app, or create (or significantly edit) a Wikipedia page. The three choices span text, audio, and video, and all three are meant to help students understand that "we're all journalists," which comes with some ethical responsibilities to present the truth as best we can. "In the old days," South said, "freedom of the press belonged to someone who owned the press, and the press was really expensive." Today, however, technology has lowered the bar. Through this assignment, which connects students to specific established communities, "students realize, I can really make a difference. I can get something out there that will live and inform people."

Connecting students with established communities can go in unexpected directions. Zoe LeBlanc, now a digital humanities developer at the University of Virginia's Scholars' Lab, served as a teaching assistant for a course on the Arab Spring in the Vanderbilt history department in 2014. She encouraged her students to tweet about the weekly readings. Thanks to a particular hashtag, one of her student's tweets went viral in Islamist circles in Saudi Arabia. She turned the retweets into a time for telling, helping students understand that the conversations they had in discussion section intersected with real communities around the world. She wanted her students to "realize that there are real people in this part of the world, that a lot of them are the same age but going through very different life experiences."[14] The viral tweet helped her students make that connection.

That tweet also demonstrated the challenge of managing privacy online. LeBlanc said she often hears the admonition, "Don't put yourself out there. You don't want to say something that's going to get you in trouble later." However, she pointed to all the online communities she belongs to as a historian. "If you're a professional and you're not engaged in scholarly or academic or professional communities," LeBlanc asked, "What does that say about you? Why aren't you there? I don't think the right answer is to always shut down and lock down, but to be really intentional about what you put out there and how you represent yourself." Like Jeff South, LeBlanc sees value in having her students participate in existing online communities for professional development as well as other reasons. Navigating those communities isn't easy, but perhaps it's in college and university settings where students should learn to do so.

Practical Advice

Taking student work public is perhaps the trickiest of technology uses discussed in this book, given the risk involved to students' privacy and reputation. The following suggestions are meant to help instructors make informed, intentional choices as they connect their students with authentic audiences.

1. Not all student work should go public. Just as actors need rehearsals before a big show and athletes need training before a big game, students need spaces to practice where they can mess up, get feedback, and improve their work. You might provide a series of small assignments that are private to the class to get students ready for a final, public project or have students revise their work one or more times before posting it online. Students who are more novice or who are tackling controversial subjects might need more private space to work than other students.

2. Consider semipublic spaces for student work. For instance, you might set up a blog for a course that's password-restricted to you, your students, and a selected number of guests—maybe outside experts, clients for a student project,

or another class of students for a course exchange. Student work doesn't need to be on the open Web to be visible to a targeted authentic audience.

3. Share only the best student work. Chris Willmott posts to YouTube only two or three top student videos out of ten or more videos produced each module. Holly Tucker and I gave all of my students the opportunity to publish on *Wonders and Marvels*, but students had to put in the effort to bring their essays up to Tucker's standards for the site. The potential for reaching an external audience will motivate students, as will the setting of high standards.

4. Check with your institution about student privacy policies. FERPA, the Family Educational Rights and Privacy Act, is the federal law that governs educational records in the United States. The fact that student X is enrolled in course Y is protected information under FERPA, which means that you can't reveal that on behalf of students; they have to choose to. Most institutions have policies that allow for student work to be made public online under certain conditions, such as allowing students to use a pseudonym or alerting students to assignment requirements for public work on the first day of class. Some institutions are more restrictive than others, however, so investigate the rules on your campus.

5. Talk to students about developing their digital professional identities. As Zoe LeBlanc noted, not having a Web presence can be a hindrance in some professions. Jeff South has his journalism students set up LinkedIn pages for themselves and link to their best published work. Having students produce quality work in public can be a way to help students build their online reputation, but students will likely need some guidance as they go about this. You might look at the Web presences of recent alumni of your institution with your students and discuss what makes them effective.

6. Prepare for negative reactions to public student work. Critique is a little easier to handle from fellow students in a course

exchange, but the comments sections on YouTube and other major websites can be brutal. Markers of students' gender, racial, or religious identity can sometimes generate biased and offensive responses, so be careful about how students present themselves in online spaces. There's value in having students share quality work online, and, as Jeff South noted, going into certain professions means dealing with hard stuff, but be ready to talk to students about these issues before, during, and after assignments.

7.   Be careful where you have students put their intellectual property. Check the terms of service for websites to see what rights those websites assert over submitted content. You and your students may not be comfortable with those terms of service in some cases. And be wary of storing the only copy of a student project on a website that might suddenly vanish. If students are using some online tool to create a product, look for ways to download or archive the work.

8.   Your local course management system probably isn't going to help you connect your students to an authentic audience. These systems are typically structured to restrict access to course materials and products to the instructor and students enrolled in the course. They're not good at opening up access even within a campus, much less to the open Web. You'll need other tools—blogs, apps, YouTube, SoundCloud—to share student work.

9.   Help your students understand their audience. At the very least, give them a description of the hypothetical audience for their work. Have students examine work produced for their target audience to reverse engineer who that audience is. If possible, have them hear from someone in that audience or someone who works with that audience regularly. Students won't benefit from the audience effect if they aren't sure who their audience is.

10. Do your part to help your students' work reach its intended audience. Share their work on your own social networks,

and look for fellow educators who might have a use for your students' projects. Reach out to authors or researchers your students have cited. Your students will be excited ("The dude from my footnotes read my paper!"), and most creators will be honored students are considering their work.

Conclusion

***

I TOOK UP photography in 2010. That was the year I read the first edition of *Presentation Zen* by Garr Reynolds. As I mentioned in the chapter on multimodal assignments, that book will change your thinking about PowerPoint presentations. For me, it was also my entry into the world of photography. One of the presentation design moves that Reynolds advocates is the use of big, beautiful photos in place of slides full of bullet points. Take the idea or concept you want to convey to your audience, find a high-quality photograph that represents that idea concretely or metaphorically, then use that photograph as your slide. During your presentation, the image complements and reinforces the story you tell with your words. Dual coding in action. I went all-in, overhauling my PowerPoint slides and spending hours on the photo-sharing site Flickr, finding Creative Commons licensed photos I could use in my presentations. The more I searched for and made use of beautiful photos, the more I wanted to make them myself.

I started taking my little point-and-shoot camera everywhere, looking for opportunities to practice taking photos. The Nashville Zoo was a favorite destination, as was Cheekwood, our local botanical gardens. If my photos from that era have merit, it's because I found interesting things to shoot, not because I had much skill! But I kept practicing. Things accelerated in February 2011 when I discovered the Daily Shoot, a Twitter account (@dailyshoot) that posted daily photography assignments for motivation and inspiration.[1] For instance, "2011/02/27: Make a photograph of something that is glowing today." Or, "2011/03/01: Find a repeating pattern today and make a photograph of it." I loved having a daily photo challenge, and I participated as often as I could, sharing my photos on Flickr and seeing how other photographers responded to the assignments as they shared their photos. (There was a Twitter hashtag for each assignment, making it easy to find posts, as well some curation magic happening on the Daily Shoot website.) I learned a lot about photography through the Daily Shoot. I learned through trial and error as I tried to get my puny camera to make the shot I wanted. I learned through observation of other photographers' work, picking up ideas about lighting and composition and subject matter. And some of the assignments involved technical terms ("2011/05/11: Make a high-key photograph today.") that I had to look up.

The Daily Shoot ran through October 2011, and I'm grateful to this day for that community for all the ways it helped me become a better photographer. That summer, I upgraded my point-and-shoot to a "real" camera, a low-end DSLR. I could make the new camera do things that my old camera just couldn't, like take a photo with a shallow depth of field, where one thing is in focus and everything in front or behind it is pleasantly out of focus. I read books about photography, I took a digital photography class at Vanderbilt, I continued sharing and viewing photos on Flickr, and I practiced . . . a lot. Somewhere along the line, I learned about photo editing, which had its own learning curve. It's still hard to look at the photos I edited in 2012, which are, shall we say, somewhat oversaturated. But I got better. So much so that I've had two paying gigs as a photographer, which makes me a professional, I guess. And I now regularly use my own photos in my presentations, bringing this story full circle.

Why am I sharing this story? I've spent years learning photography, and I'm not done yet. The same is true for my teaching. Teaching, like photography, isn't something some of us are just born to do. It's a complex set of skills that takes time and effort to develop, and we're never done learning how to teach. As you explore new teaching practices of all kinds, be intentional not only with the ways you use technology to support student learning but also with the ways you pursue your own development as a teacher. Just as I had to practice my photography, give yourself opportunities for practice and feedback. That can mean self-reflection, noting after a class session what worked and what didn't, or revisiting your teaching philosophy statement once a year to examine how your teaching has changed. Feedback from peers, including other faculty and trained staff at teaching centers, can be invaluable as we experiment with instructional practices and incorporate technology in our teaching.

Know that you'll miss the mark occasionally, and that's okay. You'll try some activity in your classroom that flops, test-drive in front of your students some new piece of technology that doesn't work, or realize halfway through an assignment that you just structured it badly. You can recover from these things, and you'll leverage that experience to the benefit of future students. Small changes over time can lead to really robust assignments and activities and a lot of confidence in your own teaching skills. Recall that Humberto Garcia didn't start out as the "blogfather" of the English department. He tried a few new things with blogs every semester, being careful not to reach too far beyond his own technical and pedagogical skills and being mindful of his own limited time. Eight semesters later, he was the guy I went to for advice on teaching with blogs. Developing one's teaching is an ongoing process, not a one-time fix.

Just as the Daily Shoot community provided me inspiration and motivation, the teaching community on your campus and beyond can be an important part of your professional growth. As Lee Shulman noted, too often "we close the classroom door and experience pedagogical solitude."[2] If instead we treat teaching as a community endeavor, we can learn from and with each other as we deepen our understanding of learning and refine our pedagogical practices. One of the best parts of my job directing a teaching center is getting to have conversations about teaching and learning with faculty and other instructors all across the disciplines. Those disciplinary differences matter to teaching, of course, but there are so many benefits from sharing our teaching experiences with each other. Teaching is a creative act, and creativity feeds on inspiration. I hope that the stories and examples in this book have provided you with inspiration for teaching with technology, and I encourage you to continue to seek out inspiration among your peers and colleagues and to share with them your teaching experiments and successes.

Technologies, particularly digital technologies, can sometimes feel so different from the kinds of teaching we're used to that we approach them with some trepidation. But technologies expand our toolbox of strategies and structures we can use to help our students learn. Figuring out how to use new technologies in intentional ways that support student learning can be challenging and can take a fair amount of time and effort, but like other ways we stretch and grow our teaching, doing so can be incredibly rewarding. A few years ago, I was putting together a talk on teaching with technology at Boise State University. I remember zooming out on the Prezi I was using as part of my presentation and realizing that almost every image I used was a representation of student work. Concept maps, Twitter posts, infographics, Wikipedia entries, collaborative bibliographies, and more. Our students can do pretty amazing things with the right tools and a little support. Technology can create new and powerful learning experiences for our students, if we're intentional about how we shape those experiences. The teaching principles discussed in this book provide some guidance, but you'll have to figure how to shape those experiences for your students. I look forward to hearing about the amazing things your students do.

Notes

Introduction

1. Derek Bruff, *Classroom Response Systems: Creating Active Learning Environments* (San Francisco: Jossey-Bass, 2009).
2. *Leading Lines* (podcast), Vanderbilt University, http://www .leadinglinespod.com.

Chapter 1

1. Daniel Schwartz and John Bransford, "A Time for Telling," *Cognition and Instruction* 16, no. 4 (1999): 475–522.
2. Bertrand Schneider, Jenelle Wallace, Paulo Blikstein, and Roy Pea, "Preparing for Future Learning with a Tangle User Interface: The Case of Neuroscience," *IEEE Transactions on Learning Technologies* 6, no. 2 (April–June 2013): 117–29.
3. Daniel Kahneman, *Thinking, Fast and Slow* (New York: Farrar, Straus, and Giroux, 2011).
4. This section adapted from Derek Bruff, "One-Best-Answer Questions: Clickers, Critical Thinking, and Legal Education," *Agile Learning* (blog), February 22, 2016, http://derekbruff.org/?p=3187.
5. That's a bit of a fib. Cheng told me that there's a rather arcane argument that works for choice D (none of the above) but he asserted that none of his students made that argument in their defense of choice D. I include this note because I hope that law educators will continue reading this book after this example.

6.   Adam Cadre, *9:05* (game), http://adamcadre.ac/if/905.html.

7.   Sam Barlow, *Her Story* (game), http://www.herstorygame.com/.

8.   RePlay Health, Tiltfactor, accessed December 5, 2018, http://www
      .replayhealth.com/.

9.   Geoff Kaufman and Mary Flanagan, "High-Low Split: Divergent
      Cognitive Construal Levels Triggered by Digital and Non-Digital
      Platforms" (paper presented at the Association for Computing
      Machinery's Computer-Human Interaction Conference, San Jose,
      CA, May 2016).

10.   Carol Dweck, *Mindset: The New Psychology of Success* (New York:
      Ballantine Books, 2008).

11.   Eric Mazur, *Peer Instruction: A User's Manual* (Upper Saddle River,
      NJ: Prentice Hall, 1997).

Chapter 2

1.   Susan Ambrose, Michael Bridges, Michele DiPietro, Marsha Lovett,
      and Marie Norman, *How Learning Works: Seven Research-Based
      Principles for Smart Teaching* (San Francisco: Jossey-Bass, 2010).

2.   Robert Talbert, *Flipped Learning: A Guide for Higher Education
      Faculty* (Sterling, VA: Stylus, 2017).

3.   Haerin Shin, "Flipping the Flipped Classroom: The Beauty of
      Spontaneous and Instantaneous Close Reading," *National Teaching
      and Learning Forum* 24, no. 4 (May 2015): 1–4.

4.   Derek Bruff, "Humberto Garcia," Episode 22, *Leading Lines*,
      Vanderbilt University, podcast audio, August 7, 2017, http://
      leadinglinespod.com/episodes/episode-022-humberto-garcia/.

5.   Stacey Johnson, "Elizabeth Self," Episode 25, *Leading Lines*,
      Vanderbilt University, podcast audio, September 18, 2017, http://
      leadinglinespod.com/episodes/episode-025-elizabeth-self/.

6.   Grace Tatter, "Teacher Training Programs Strive to Bridge Culture,
      Racial Gaps in the Classroom," *Chalkbeat*, July 15, 2015, https://
      www.chalkbeat.org/posts/tn/2015/07/22/tennessee-teacher
      -training-programs-strive-to-bridge-culture-racial-gaps-in-the
      -classroom/.

7.   Johnson, "Elizabeth Self."

8.   Johnson, "Elizabeth Self."

9.   Clifford Anderson, "Kathryn Tomasek," Episode 11, *Leading Lines*, Vanderbilt University, podcast audio, January 16, 2017, http://leadinglinespod.com/episodes/episode-011-kathryn-tomasek/.

10.   Text Encoding Initiative, http://www.tei-c.org/.

11.   "Eliza Baylies Chapin Wheaton Grand Tour of Europe 1862 Travel Journal," TAPAS Project, updated October 22, 2015, http://tapasproject.org/elizawheatonpapers/files/1862-journal.

12.   Anderson, "Kathryn Tomasek."

13.   Kathryn Tomasek, Scott Hamlin, Zephorene Stickney, and Megan Wheaton-Book, "Discipline-Specific Learning and Collaboration in the Wheaton College Digital History Project," *Academic Commons*, August 25, 2015, http://www.academiccommons.org/2014/08/25/discipline-specific-learning-and-collaboration-in-the-wheaton-college-digital-history-project/.

14.   "TILE—Transform, Interact, Learn, Engage," University of Iowa Information Technology Services, https://its.uiowa.edu/tile; Susan Grajek, *Higher Education's Top 10 Strategic Technologies for 2017*, research report (Louisville, CO: EDUCAUSE Center for Analysis and Research, March 2017).

15.   Paul Baepler, J. D. Walker, D. Christopher Brooks, Kem Saichaie, and Christina Petersen, *A Guide to Teaching in Active Learning Classrooms: History, Research, and Practice* (Sterling, VA: Stylus, 2016).

16.   Derek Bruff, "Cornelia Lang," Episode 32, *Leading Lines*, Vanderbilt University, podcast audio, January 2, 2018, http://leadinglinespod.com/episodes/episode-32-cornelia-lang/.

17.   Aimee Whiteside, D. Christopher Brooks, and J. Walker, "Making the Case for Space: Three Years of Empirical Research on Learning Environments," *EDUCAUSE Quarterly* 33 (September 2010).

18.   Scott Freeman, Sarah Eddy, Miles McDonough, Michelle Smith, Nnadozie Okoroafor, Hannah Jordt, and Mary Pat Wenderoth, "Active Learning Increases Student Performance in Science, Engineering, and Mathematics," *Proceedings of the National Academy of Science* 111, no. 23 (June 2014): 8410–15.

19.   Carl Wieman, "Large-Scale Comparison of Science Teaching Methods Sends Clear Message," *Proceedings of the National Academy of Science* 111, no. 23 (June 2014): 8319–20.

20.   Derek Bruff, "In Defense of Continuous Exposition by the Teacher," *Agile Learning* (blog), September 15, 2015, http://derekbruff.org /?p=3126.

21.   Mark Sample, October 18, 2015, comment on Bruff, "In Defense," http://derekbruff.org/?p=3126#comment-60491.

22.   Elizabeth Barkley, *Student Engagement Techniques: A Handbook for College Faculty* (San Francisco: Jossey-Bass, 2009); Heather Macpherson Parrott and Elizabeth Cherry, "Using Structured Reading Groups to Facilitate Deep Learning," *Teaching Sociology* 39, no. 4 (September 2011): 354–70.

23.   Lendol Calder, "Uncoverage: Toward a Signature Pedagogy of the History Survey," *Journal of American History* 92, no. 4 (March 2006): 1358–70.

Chapter 3

1.   Sophie Bruff, "Sonder," YouTube, March 22, 2017, https://www .youtube.com/watch?v=WCZ7jxRTFU4.

2.   Vashi Nedomansky, "Shooting Ratios of Feature Films," *VashiVisuals* (blog), February 6, 2016, http://vashivisuals.com /shooting-ratios-of-feature-films/.

3.   Randall Bass, "Disrupting Ourselves: The Problem of Learning in Higher Education," *EDUCAUSE Review* 47, no. 2 (March 2012).

4.   Randall Bass, "The Problem of Learning in a Post-Course Era" (presented at the EDUCAUSE Learning Initiative Annual Meeting, New Orleans, LA, February 2011).

5.   Cyprien Lomas, "7 Things You Should Know about Social Bookmarking," EDUCAUSE Learning Initiative, May 1, 2005, https://library.educause.edu/resources/2005/5/7-things-you -should-know-about-social-bookmarking.

6.   Derek Bruff, "Math 1111: Cryptography," Diigo, updated December 1, 2018, https://groups.diigo.com/group/fwyscrypto.

7.   Center for the Integration of Research, Teaching, and Learning
      MOOC, "Margaret Rubega, Ornithology," video, August 31,
      2015, https://www.youtube.com/watch?v=ik0Wa1bWmP4.

8.   John Bransford, Ann Brown, and Rodney Cocking, *How People
      Learn: Brain, Mind, Experience, and School* (Washington, DC:
      National Academies Press, 2000).

9.   Kim Smith, "The Twitter Experiment: Twitter in the Classroom,"
      YouTube, May 2, 2009, https://www.youtube.com/watch?v
      =6WPVWDkF7U8.

10.   Derek Bruff, "Backchannel in Education: Nine Uses," *Agile
      Learning* (blog), January 21, 2010, http://derekbruff.org
      /?p=472.

11.   Mark Sample, "Tracking Moves on the Classroom Backchannel
      with Storify," *ProfHacker* (blog), December 1, 2011, https://www
      .chronicle.com/blogs/profhacker/tracking-moves-on-the
      -classroom-backchannel-with-storify/37458.

12.   Leigh Wright, "Tweet Me a Story," in *Web Writing: How and Why
      for Liberal Arts Teaching and Learning*, ed. Jack Dougherty and
      Tennyson O'Donnell (Ann Arbor: University of Michigan Press,
      2014).

13.   Paula Soneral and Sara Wyse, "A SCALE-UP Mock-up:
      Comparison of Student Learning Gains in High-Tech and Low-
      Tech Active Learning Classrooms," *CBE—Life Sciences Education*
      16, no. 1 (Spring 2017).

14.   Ian Beatty, William Leonard, William Gerace, and Robert
      Dufresne, "Question Driven Instruction: Teaching Science (Well)
      with an Audience Response Systems," in *Audience Response
      Systems in Higher Education: Application and Uses*, ed. David
      Banks (Hershey, PA: Information Science Publishing, 2006).

15.   Bruff, *Teaching with Classroom Response Systems*.

16.   Grant Wiggins and Jay McTighe, *Understanding by Design*, 2nd
      ed. (Alexandria, VA: Association for Supervision and Curriculum
      Development, 2005).

17.   Barbara Walvoord and Virginia Johnson Anderson, *Effective
      Grading: A Tool for Learning and Assessment in College*, 2nd ed.
      (San Francisco: Jossey-Bass, 2009).

Chapter 4

1.   Bransford, Brown, and Cocking, *How People Learn*.

2.   Cory Doctor, "How a Mathematician Teaches *Little Brother* to a First-Year Seminar," *BoingBoing* (blog), October 21, 2015, http://boingboing.net/2015/10/21/how-a-mathematician-teaches.html.

3.   See Derek Bruff (@derekbruff), "@doctorow Thanks for sharing my debate map activity! Glad you thought it interesting. One Question: 'surveillance' or 'security'?," Twitter, October 21, 2015, 11:07 a.m., https://twitter.com/derekbruff/status/656864312498245632, and subsequent replies.

4.   Christine D'Onofrio, "Linking Lecture to Lab," Teaching Dossier Appendix, accessed December 7, 2018, https://blogs.ubc.ca/donofrio/linking-lecture-to-lab/.

5.   John Cao, "Synthesis Map Complete Version," Prezi, June 19, 2014, https://prezi.com/tp6jcnrnlh3a/synthesis-map-complete-version/.

6.   Ryan Ortega and Cynthia Brame, "The Synthesis Map Is a Multidimensional Educational Tool That Provides Insight into Students' Mental Models and Promotes Students' Synthetic Knowledge Generation," *CBE—Life Sciences Education* 14 (Summer 2015): 1–11.

7.   Ortega and Brame, "The Synthesis Map," 2.

8.   Yong Lee, "Mapping Character Development across Time with Prezi Meeting," *The Prospect* (blog), September 13, 2011, blogs.commons.georgetown.edu/blog/archives/723.

9.   Erin Sells, "Mapping Novels with Google Earth," *ProfHacker* (blog), April 6, 2011, https://www.chronicle.com/blogs/profhacker/mapping-novels/32528.

10.   "Guiding Principles," Writing and Communication Program, Georgia Tech, accessed December 7, 2018, https://wcprogram.lmc.gatech.edu/guiding-principles/.

11.   Amanda Golden, "Mapping *Jacob's Room*," *Tech Style* (blog), November 12, 2013, http://techstyle.lmc.gatech.edu/mapping-jacobs-room/.

12.   Bryan Lowe, "Technological Tools and Methods for Teaching Premodern Japanese Materials," *Vanderbilt Center for Teaching Blog*

(blog), November 28, 2017, https://cft.vanderbilt.edu/2017/11 /technological-tools-and-methods-for-teaching-premodern -japanese-materials-bryan-lowe/.

13. Patrick Meng, "Nippon," Tiki-Toki, accessed December 7, 2018, http://www.tiki-toki.com/timeline/entry/580964/Nippon/.

14. Lowe, "Technological Tools and Methods."

15. Danielle Picard and Derek Bruff, "Digital Timelines," Vanderbilt Center for Teaching, 2016, https://cft.vanderbilt.edu/guides-sub -pages/digital-timelines/. For more examples of teaching with timelines, see the chapter on learning communities, as well as the Vanderbilt Center for Teaching's teaching guide on digital timelines.

16. Kaufman and Flanagan, "High-Low Split."

17. Edward Tufte, *The Visual Display of Quantitative Information*, 2nd ed. (Cheshire, CT: Graphics Press, 2001); Dan Roam, *The Back of the Napkin: Solving Problems and Selling Ideas with Pictures*, expanded ed. (New York: Penguin Group, 2010).

18. Ambrose et al., *How Learning Works*, 53.

Chapter 5

1. Harold Pashler, Mark McDaniel, Doug Rohrer, and Robert Bjork, "Learning Styles: Concepts and Evidence," *Psychological Sciences in the Public Interest* 9, no. 3 (December 2008): 105–19.

2. Beth Rogowsky, Barbara Calhoun, and Paula Tallal, "Matching Learning Style to Instructional Method: Effects on Comprehension," *Journal of Educational Psychology* 107, no. 1 (2015): 64–78. See also Abby Knoll, Hajime Otani, Reid Skeel, and K. Roger Van Horn, "Learning Style, Judgements of Learning, and Learning of Verbal and Visual Information," *British Journal of Psychology* 108, no. 3 (2017): 544–63.

3. Cedar Riener and Daniel Willingham, "The Myth of Learning Styles," *Change* 42, no. 5 (September/October 2010): 32–35.

4. Linda Nilson, *Teaching at Its Best: A Research-Based Resource for College Instructors*, 4th ed. (San Francisco: Jossey-Bass, 2016).

5. This paragraph adapted from Derek Bruff, "Learning Styles: Fact and Fiction (#lilly10)," *Agile Learning* (blog), December 6, 2010, https://derekbruff.org/?p=590.

6. Allan Paivio, *Mind and Its Evolution: A Dual Coding Theoretical Approach* (New York: Lawrence Erlbaum Associates, 2007). See also Richard Mayer, *Multimedia Learning*, 2nd ed. (Cambridge: Cambridge University Press, 2009).

7. Garr Reynolds, *Presentation Zen: Simple Ideas on Presentation Design and Delivery*, 2nd ed. (Berkeley, CA: New Riders Press, 2012).

8. Derek Bruff, "Students as Producers: Collaborating Toward Deeper Learning," in *Scholarship in the Sandbox: Academic Libraries as Laboratories, Forums, and Archives for Student Work*, ed. Cindy Pierard, Amy Jackson, and Suzanne Schadl (Chicago: Association of College and Research Libraries, 2019).

9. Derek Bruff, "Tia Smith," Episode 49, *Leading Lines*, Vanderbilt University, podcast audio, December 3, 2018, http://leadinglinespod.com/episodes/episode-049tia-smith/.

10. This section adapted from Derek Bruff, "A Crowdsourced Rubric for Evaluating Infographics," *Agile Learning* (blog), April 11, 2012, http://derekbruff.org/?p=2081.

11. Hans Rosling, "Let My Dataset Change Your Mindset," TED.com, June 2009, https://www.ted.com/talks/hans_rosling_at_state.

12. Jung Min Shin, *The Velveteen Rabbit*: Exploring the Boundary Between the Real and Unreal, 2014, http://jasmine138.wixsite.com/velveteenrabbit.

13. Derek Bruff, "Haerin Shin," Episode 24, *Leading Lines*, Vanderbilt University, podcast audio, September 4, 2017, http://leadinglinespod.com/episodes/episode-024-haerin-shin/.

14. StoryCenter, https://www.storycenter.org/.

15. Bernard Robin, "Digital Storytelling: A Powerful Technology Tool for the 21st Century Classroom," *Theory into Practice* 47, no. 3 (2008): 220–28.

16. Kylie Korsnack, "Revisiting the Pedagogy Project and Reimagining Revision," *HASTAC Blog* (blog), January 24, 2017, https://www.hastac.org/blogs/kyliejk/2017/01/24/16-revisiting-pedagogy-project-and-re-imagining-revision.

17. Zachary Ellington, "The Adventures of an Outcast," accessed December 7, 2018, https://writer.inklestudios.com/stories/9z3r.

18. Twine, http://twinery.org/.

19. Derek Bruff, "Gilbert Gonzales," Episode 27, *Leading Lines*, Vanderbilt University, podcast audio, October 16, 2017, http://leadinglinespod.com/episodes/episode-027-gilbert-gonzales/.

20. *Health Policy Radio with Gilbert Gonzales* (podcast), https://soundcloud.com/user-175461561.

21. *One-Time Pod* (podcast), http://derekbruff.org/blogs/fywscrypto/historical-crypto/one-time-pod/.

22. Augie Phillips, "Miocene," YouTube, April 21, 2015, https://www.youtube.com/watch?v=WDaopt5dYBI.

23. For examples, see the podcast VandyVox, http://vandyvox.com/, produced by the Vanderbilt University Center for Teaching and Vanderbilt Student Media.

24. Craig Mertler, "Designing Scoring Rubrics for Your Classroom," *Practical Assessment, Research and Evaluation* 7, no. 25 (December 2001): 1–10.

25. Thomas J. Tobin and Kirsten T. Behling, *Reach Everyone, Teach Everyone: Universal Design for Learning in Higher Education* (Morgantown: West Virginia University Press, 2018).

Chapter 6

1. Constance Steinkuehler and Sean Duncan, "Scientific Habits of Mind in Virtual Worlds," *Journal of Science Education and Technology* 17, no. 6 (December 2008): 530–43.

2. Richard Ryan and Edward Deci, "Self-Determination Theory and the Facilitation of Intrinsic Motivation, Social Development, and Well-Being," *American Psychologist* 55, no. 1 (January 2000): 68–78.

3. George Kuh, *High-Impact Educational Practices: What They Are, Who Has Access to Them, and Why They Matter* (Washington, DC: Association of American Colleges and Universities, 2008); Aaron Brower and Karen Kurotsuchi Inkelas, "Living-Learning Programs: One High-Impact Educational Practice We Know a Lot About," *Liberal Education* 96, no. 2 (Spring 2010).

4.   Ann Austin, Henry Campa III, Christine Pfund, Donald Gillian-Daniel, Robert Mathieu, and Judith Stoddart, "Preparing STEM Doctoral Students for Future Faculty Careers," *New Directions in Teaching and Learning* 117 (March 2009): 83–95.

5.   Erika Grundstrom, *Astro2110: The Solar System* (blog), https://my.vanderbilt.edu/astro201solarsys/.

6.   Kendra Oliver and Richard Coble, "Teaching with Blogs," Vanderbilt Center for Teaching, 2016, https://cft.vanderbilt.edu/teaching-with-blogs/.

7.   Jeff Young, "Actually Going to Class, for a Specific Course? How 20th-Century," *Chronicle of Higher Education*, February 27, 2011, https://www.chronicle.com/article/Actually-Going-to-Class-How/126519.

8.   spacedout512, "Gravitational Waves!!!!," *Spaced Out* (blog), February 15, 2016, https://spacedout512.wordpress.com/2016/02/15/gravitational-waves/.

9.   Rani Banjarian, "love is in the spacetime," *Beyond the Move* (blog), February 17, 2016, https://beyondthemove.wordpress.com/2016/02/17/love-is-in-the-spacetime/.

10.   Rani Banjarian, March 1, 2016, comment on Banjarian, "love is in the spacetime," https://beyondthemove.wordpress.com/2016/02/17/love-is-in-the-spacetime/#comment-14.

11.   Derek Bruff, "Enoch Hale," Episode 19, *Leading Lines*, Vanderbilt University, podcast audio, May 15, 2017, http://leadinglinespod.com/episodes/episode-019-enoch-hale/.

12.   Elizabeth Meadows, "Love and Marriage," Tiki-Toki, 2014, http://www.tiki-toki.com/timeline/entry/227613/Love-and-Marriage/.

13.   Keith Weghorst, "Democracy in Time," Witness Democracy, accessed December 8, 2018, https://www.witnessdemocracy.com/democracy-in-time.html.

14.   Derek Bruff, "Timelines, EdTech, and Thin Slices of Student Learning," *Agile Learning* (blog), February 10, 2016, http://derekbruff.org/?p=3171.

15.   Jonathan Neville, "The Age of Reason (Thomas Paine) 60 Second Plot Summary," 2015, https://vimeo.com/140381669.

16. Robin DeRosa, ed., *The Open Anthology of Earlier American Literature*, October 13, 2015, https://openamlit.pressbooks.com/.

17. OpenStax, Rice University, https://openstax.org/.

18. Robin DeRosa, "My Open Textbook: Pedagogy and Practice," *actualham* (blog), May 18, 2016, http://robinderosa.net/uncategorized/my-open-textbook-pedagogy-and-practice/.

19. Remi Kalir, "Moderating Entities and Annotation as Meaningful Engagement," *Remi(x)Learning* (blog), May 13, 2017, https://remikalir.com/projects/moderating-entities-and-annotation-as-meaningful-engagement/.

20. Jay Howard, *Discussion in the College Classroom: Getting Your Students Engaged and Participating in Person and Online* (San Francisco: Jossey-Bass, 2015).

21. Elaine Seymour and Nancy Hewitt, *Talking about Leaving: Why Undergraduates Leave the Sciences* (Boulder, CO: Westview Press, 1997).

22. Claude Steele, *Whistling Vivaldi: How Stereotypes Affect Us and What We Can Do* (New York: Norton, 2010).

23. Lucy Appert, Christine Simonian Bean, Amanda Irvin, Amanda Jungels, Suzanna Klaf, and Mark Phillipson, "Guide to Inclusive Teaching," Columbia University Center for Teaching and Learning, 2018, https://ctl.columbia.edu/resources-and-technology/inclusive-teaching-guide/.

24. Geoffrey Cohen, Claude Steele, and Lee Ross, "The Mentor's Dilemma: Providing Critical Feedback across the Racial Divide," *Personality and Social Psychology Bulletin* 25, no. 1 (October 1999): 1302–18.

25. Maha Bali, "Open on Whose Terms?," *ProfHacker* (blog), May 2, 2017, https://www.chronicle.com/blogs/profhacker/open-on-whose-terms/63986.

26. Walvoord and Anderson, *Effective Grading*.

Chapter 7

1. Richard Light, *Making the Most of College: Students Speak Their Minds* (Cambridge, MA: Harvard University Press, 2001).

2.   Holly Tucker, ed., "Cryptography / Vanderbilt," *Wonders and Marvels* (blog), updated November 2014, http://www .wondersandmarvels.com/category/cryptography-vanderbilt.

3.   Alberto Perez, "How the U. S. Cracked Japan's Purple Encryption Machine at the Dawn of World War II," io9, March 22, 2013, https://io9.gizmodo.com/how-the-u-s-cracked-japans-purple -encryption-machine-458385664.

4.   Randall Bass and Heidi Elmendorf, "Designing for Difficulty: Social Pedagogies as a Framework for Course Design," Teagle Foundation White Paper, 2012, https://blogs.commons .georgetown.edu/bassr/social-pedagogies/.

5.   Mark Carnes, *Minds on Fire: How Role-Immersion Games Transform College* (Cambridge, MA: Harvard University Press, 2014).

6.   Chris Willmott, BioethicsBytes, https://www.youtube.com/user /BioethicsBytes/videos.

7.   Chris Willmott, "Teaching Bioethics via the Production of Student-Generated Videos," *Journal of Biological Education* 49, no. 2 (2014): 127–38.

8.   Matt Lavin and Bridget Draxler, "Social Annotating and Skype: An Experimental Course Exchange," *HASTAC Blog* (blog), February 17, 2014, https://www.hastac.org/blogs/bridget -draxler/2014/02/17/06-social-annotating-and-skype -experimental-course-exchange.

9.   Derek Bruff, "Tim Foster," Episode 13, *Leading Lines*, Vanderbilt University, podcast audio, February 20, 2017, http:// leadinglinespod.com/episodes/episode-013-tim-foster/.

10.   "Nashville," Wikipédia, updated November 13, 2018, https:// pt.wikipedia.org/wiki/Nashville.

11.   Scott Jaschik, "A Stand against Wikipedia," *Inside Higher Ed*, January 26, 2007, http://www.insidehighered.com/news /2007/01/26/wiki; Gayathri Narasimham, "Carwil Bjork-James," Episode 18, *Leading Lines*, Vanderbilt University, podcast audio, May 1, 2017, http://leadinglinespod.com/episodes/episode-018 -carwil-bjork-james/.

12. Maude Gauthier and Kim Sawchuk, "Not Notable Enough: Feminism and Expertise in Wikipedia," *Journal of Communication and Critical/Cultural Studies* 14, no. 4 (2014): 385–402.

13. VCU Capital News Service, https://vcucns.com/.

14. Derek Bruff, "Zoe LeBlanc," Episode 8, *Leading Lines*, Vanderbilt University, podcast audio, November 21, 2016, http://leadinglinespod.com/episodes/episode-008-zoe-leblanc/.

Conclusion

1. Daily Shoot (@dailyshoot), https://twitter.com/dailyshoot.

2. Lee Shulman, "Teaching as Community Property: Putting an End to Pedagogical Solitude," *Change* 25, no. 6 (November 1993): 6–7.

References

Ambrose, Susan, Michael Bridges, Michele DiPietro, Marsha Lovett, and Marie Norman. *How Learning Works: Seven Research-Based Principles for Smart Teaching*. San Francisco: Jossey-Bass, 2010.

Anderson, Clifford. "Kathryn Tomasek." Episode 11. *Leading Lines*. Vanderbilt University. Podcast audio, January 16, 2017. http://leadinglinespod.com/episodes/episode-011-kathryn-tomasek/.

Appert, Lucy, Christine Simonian Bean, Amanda Irvin, Amanda Jungels, Suzanna Klaf, and Mark Phillipson. "Guide to Inclusive Teaching." Columbia University Center for Teaching and Learning. 2018. https://ctl.columbia.edu/resources-and-technology/inclusive-teaching-guide/.

Austin, Ann, Henry Campa III, Christine Pfund, Donald Gillian-Daniel, Robert Mathieu, and Judith Stoddart. "Preparing STEM Doctoral Students for Future Faculty Careers." *New Directions in Teaching and Learning* 117 (March 2009): 83–95.

Baepler, Paul, J. D. Walker, D. Christopher Brooks, Kem Saichaie, and Christina Petersen. *A Guide to Teaching in Active Learning Classrooms: History, Research, and Practice*. Sterling, VA: Stylus, 2016.

Bali, Maha. "Open on Whose Terms?" *ProfHacker* (blog). *Chronicle of Higher Education*. May 2, 2017. https://www.chronicle.com/blogs/profhacker/open-on-whose-terms/63986.

Barkley, Elizabeth. *Student Engagement Techniques: A Handbook for College Faculty*. San Francisco: Jossey-Bass, 2009.

Bass, Randall. "Disrupting Ourselves: The Problem of Learning in Higher Education." *EDUCAUSE Review* 47, no. 2 (March 2012).

Bass, Randall. "The Problem of Learning in a Post-Course Era."
    Presented at the EDUCAUSE Learning Initiative Annual Meeting,
    New Orleans, February 2011.

Bass, Randall, and Heidi Elmendorf. "Designing for Difficulty:
    Social Pedagogies as a Framework for Course Design." Teagle
    Foundation White Paper. 2012. https://blogs.commons
    .georgetown.edu/bassr/social-pedagogies/.

Beatty, Ian, William Leonard, William Gerace, and Robert Dufresne.
    "Question Driven Instruction: Teaching Science (Well) with an
    Audience Response System." In *Audience Response Systems in
    Higher Education: Applications and Uses*, edited by David Banks.
    Hershey, PA: Information Science Publishing, 2006.

Bransford, John, Ann Brown, and Rodney Cocking. *How People Learn:
    Brain, Mind, Experience, and School*. Washington, DC: National
    Academies Press, 2000.

Brower, Aaron, and Karen Kurotsuchi Inkelas. "Living-Learning
    Programs: One High-Impact Educational Practice We Know a Lot
    About." *Liberal Education* 96, no. 2 (Spring 2010).

Bruff, Derek. "Backchannel in Education: Nine Uses." *Agile Learning*
    (blog). January 21, 2010. http://derekbruff.org/?p=472.

Bruff, Derek. "In Defense of Continuous Exposition by the Teacher."
    Agile Learning (blog). September 15, 2015. http://derekbruff
    .org/?p=3126.

Bruff, Derek. "Students as Producers: Collaborating toward Deeper
    Learning." In *Scholarship in the Sandbox: Academic Libraries as
    Laboratories, Forums, and Archives for Student Work*, edited by
    Cindy Pierard, Amy Jackson, and Suzanne Schadl. Chicago:
    Association of College and Research Libraries, 2019.

Bruff, Derek. *Teaching with Classroom Response Systems: Creating
    Active Learning Environments*. San Francisco: Jossey-Bass, 2009.

Bruff, Derek. "Timelines, EdTech, and Thin Slices of Student
    Learning." *Agile Learning* (blog). February 10, 2016. http://
    derekbruff.org/?p=3171.

Calder, Lendol. "Uncoverage: Toward a Signature Pedagogy of the
    History Survey." *Journal of American History* 92, no. 4 (March
    2006): 1358–70.

Carnes, Mark. *Minds on Fire: How Role-Immersion Games Transform College*. Cambridge, MA: Harvard University Press, 2014.

Center for the Integration of Research, Teaching, and Learning MOOC. "Margaret Rubega, Ornithology." YouTube. August 31, 2015. https://www.youtube.com/watch?v=ik0Wa1bWmP4.

Cohen, Geoffrey, Claude Steele, and Lee Ross. "The Mentor's Dilemma: Providing Critical Feedback across the Racial Divide." *Personality and Social Psychology Bulletin* 25, no. 1 (October 1999): 1302–18.

DeRosa, Robin. "My Open Textbook: Pedagogy and Practice." *actualham* (blog). May 18, 2016. http://robinderosa.net /uncategorized/my-open-textbook-pedagogy-and-practice/.

D'Onofrio, Christine. "Linking Lecture to Lab." Teaching Dossier Appendix. Accessed December 7, 2018. https://blogs.ubc.ca /donofrio/linking-lecture-to-lab/.

Dweck, Carol. *Mindset: The New Psychology of Success*. New York: Ballantine Books, 2008.

Freeman, Scott, Sarah Eddy, Miles McDonough, Michelle Smith, Nnadozie Okoroafor, Hannah Jordt, and Mary Pat Wenderoth. "Active Learning Increases Student Performance in Science, Engineering, and Mathematics." *Proceedings of the National Academy of Science* 111, no. 23 (June 2014): 8410–15.

Gauthier, Maude, and Kim Sawchuk. "Not Notable Enough: Feminism and Expertise in Wikipedia." *Journal of Communication and Critical/Cultural Studies* 14, no. 4 (2014): 385–402.

Golden, Amanda. "Mapping *Jacob's Room*." *Tech Style* (blog). November 12, 2013. http://techstyle.lmc.gatech.edu /mapping-jacobs-room/.

Grajek, Susan. *Higher Education's Top 10 Strategic Technologies for 2017*. Research report. Louisville, CO: EDUCAUSE Center for Analysis and Research, March 2017.

Howard, Jay. *Discussion in the College Classroom: Getting Your Students Engaged and Participating in Person and Online*. San Francisco: Jossey-Bass, 2015.

Jaschik, Scott. "A Stand against Wikipedia." *Inside Higher Ed*. January 26, 2007, http://www.insidehighered.com/news/2007/01/26 /wiki.

Johnson, Stacey. "Elizabeth Self." Episode 25. *Leading Lines*. Vanderbilt University. Podcast audio, September 18, 2017. http://leadinglinespod.com/episodes/episode-025-elizabeth-self/.

Kahneman, Daniel. *Thinking, Fast and Slow*. New York: Farrar, Straus, and Giroux, 2011.

Kalir, Remi. "Moderating Entities and Annotation as Meaningful Engagement." *Remi(x)Learning* (blog). May 13, 2017. https://remikalir.com/projects/moderating-entities-and-annotation-as-meaningful-engagement/.

Kaufman, Geoff, and Mary Flanagan. "High-Low Split: Divergent Cognitive Construal Levels Triggered by Digital and Non-Digital Platforms." Paper presented at the Association for Computing Machinery Computer-Human Interaction Conference, San Jose, CA, May 2016.

Knoll, Abby, Hajime Otani, Reid Skeel, and K. Roger Van Horn. "Learning Style, Judgements of Learning, and Learning of Visual and Verbal Information." *British Journal of Psychology* 108, no. 3 (2017): 544–63.

Korsnack, Kylie. "Revisiting the Pedagogy Project and Reimagining Revision." *HASTAC Blog* (blog). January 24, 2017. https://www.hastac.org/blogs/kyliejk/2017/01/24/16-revisiting-pedagogy-project-and-re-imagining-revision.

Kuh, George. *High-Impact Educational Practices: What They Are, Who Has Access to Them, and Why They Matter*. Washington, DC: Association of American Colleges and Universities, 2008.

Lavin, Matt, and Bridget Draxler. "Social Annotating and Skype: An Experimental Course Exchange." *HASTAC Blog* (blog). February 17, 2014. https://www.hastac.org/blogs/bridget-draxler/2014/02/17/06-social-annotating-and-skype-experimental-course-exchange.

Lee, Yong. "Mapping Character Development across Time with Prezi Meeting." *The Prospect* (blog). September 13, 2011. blogs.commons.georgetown.edu/blog/archives/723.

Light, Richard. *Making the Most of College: Students Speak Their Minds*. Cambridge, MA: Harvard University Press, 2001.

Lomas, Cyprien. "7 Things You Should Know about Social Bookmarking." EDUCAUSE Learning Initiative. May 1, 2005. https://library.educause.edu/resources/2005/5/7-things-you -should-know-about-social-bookmarking.

Lowe, Bryan. "Technological Tools and Methods for Teaching Premodern Japanese Materials." *Vanderbilt Center for Teaching Blog* (blog). November 28, 2017. https://cft.vanderbilt .edu/2017/11/technological-tools-and-methods-for-teaching -premodern-japanese-materials-bryan-lowe/.

Mayer, Richard. *Multimedia Learning*. 2nd ed. Cambridge: Cambridge University Press, 2009.

Mazur, Eric. *Peer Instruction: A User's Manual*. Upper Saddle River, NJ: Prentice Hall, 1997.

Mertler, Craig. "Designing Scoring Rubrics for Your Classroom." *Practical Assessment, Research and Evaluation* 7, no. 25 (December 2001): 1–10.

Narasimham, Gayathri. "Carwil Bjork-James." Episode 18. *Leading Lines*. Vanderbilt University. Podcast audio, May 1, 2017. http:// leadinglinespod.com/episodes/episode-018-carwil-bjork-james/.

Nedomansky, Vashi. "Shooting Ratios of Feature Films." *VashiVisuals* (blog). February 6, 2016. http://vashivisuals.com/shooting-ratios -of-feature-films/.

Nilson, Linda. *Teaching at Its Best: A Research-Based Resource for College Instructors*. 4th ed. San Francisco: Jossey-Bass, 2016.

Oliver, Kendra, and Richard Coble. "Teaching with Blogs." Vanderbilt Center for Teaching. 2016. https://cft.vanderbilt.edu/teaching -with-blogs/.

Ortega, Ryan, and Cynthia Brame. "The Synthesis Map Is a Multidimensional Educational Tool That Provides Insight into Students' Mental Models and Promotes Students' Synthetic Knowledge Generation." *CBE—Life Sciences Education* 14 (Summer 2015): 1–11.

Paivio, Allan. *Mind and Its Evolution: A Dual Coding Theoretical Approach*. New York: Lawrence Erlbaum Associates, 2007.

Parrott, Heather Macpherson, and Elizabeth Cherry. "Using

Structured Reading Groups to Facilitate Deep Learning." *Teaching Sociology* 39, no. 4 (September 2011): 354–70.

Pashler, Harold, Mark McDaniel, Doug Rohrer, and Robert Bjork. "Learning Styles: Concepts and Evidence." *Psychological Sciences in the Public Interest* 9, no. 3 (December 2008): 105–19.

Picard, Danielle, and Derek Bruff. "Digital Timelines." Vanderbilt Center for Teaching. 2016. https://cft.vanderbilt.edu/guides-sub -pages/digital-timelines/.

Reynolds, Garr. *Presentation Zen: Simple Ideas on Presentation Design and Delivery*. 2nd ed. Berkeley, CA: New Riders Press, 2012.

Riener, Cedar, and Daniel Willingham. "The Myth of Learning Styles." *Change* 42, no. 5 (September/October 2010): 32–35.

Roam, Dan. *The Back of the Napkin: Solving Problems and Selling Ideas with Pictures*. Expanded ed. New York: Penguin, 2010.

Robin, Bernard. "Digital Storytelling: A Powerful Technology Tool for the 21st Century Classroom." *Theory into Practice* 47, no. 3 (2008): 220–28.

Rogowsky, Beth, Barbara Calhoun, and Paula Tallal. "Matching Learning Style to Instructional Method: Effects on Comprehension." *Journal of Educational Psychology* 107, no. 1 (2015): 64–78.

Ryan, Richard, and Edward Deci. "Self-Determination Theory and the Facilitation of Intrinsic Motivation, Social Development, and Well-Being." *American Psychologist* 55, no. 1 (January 2000): 68–78.

Sample, Mark. "Tracking Moves on the Classroom Backchannel with Storify." *ProfHacker* (blog). *Chronicle of Higher Education*. December 1, 2011. https://www.chronicle.com/blogs/profhacker /tracking-moves-on-the-classroom-backchannel-with-storify /37458.

Schneider, Bertrand, Jenelle Wallace, Paulo Blikstein, and Roy Pea. "Preparing for Future Learning with a Tangle User Interface: The Case of Neuroscience." *IEEE Transactions on Learning Technologies* 6, no. 2 (April–June 2013): 117–29.

Schwartz, Daniel, and John Bransford. "A Time for Telling." *Cognition and Instruction* 16, no. 4 (1999): 475–522.

Sells, Erin. "Mapping Novels with Google Earth." *ProfHacker* (blog). *Chronicle of Higher Education*. April 6, 2011. https://www.chronicle.com/blogs/profhacker/mapping-novels/32528.

Seymour, Elaine, and Nancy Hewitt. *Talking about Learning: Why Undergraduates Leave the Sciences*. Boulder, CO: Westview Press, 1997.

Shin, Haerin. "Flipping the Flipped Classroom: The Beauty of Spontaneous and Instantaneous Close Reading." *National Teaching and Learning Forum* 24, no. 4 (May 2015): 1–4.

Shulman, Lee. "Teaching as Community Property: Putting an End to Pedagogical Solitude." *Change* 25, no. 6 (November 1993): 6–7.

Smith, Kim. "The Twitter Experiment: Twitter in the Classroom." YouTube. May 2, 2009. https://www.youtube.com/watch?v=6WPVWDkF7U8.

Soneral, Paula, and Sara Wyse. "A SCALE-UP Mock-up: Comparison of Student Learning Gains in High-Tech and Low-Tech Active Learning Environments." *CBE—Life Sciences Education* 16, no. 1 (Spring 2017).

Steele, Claude. *Whistling Vivaldi: How Stereotypes Affect Us and What We Can Do*. New York: Norton, 2010.

Steinkuehler, Constance, and Sean Duncan. "Scientific Habits of Mind in Virtual Worlds." *Journal of Science Education and Technology* 17, no. 6 (December 2008): 530–43.

Talbert, Robert. *Flipped Learning: A Guide for Higher Education Faculty*. Sterling, VA: Stylus, 2017.

Tatter, Grace. "Teacher Training Programs Strive to Bridge Culture, Racial Gaps in the Classroom." *Chalkbeat*, July 15, 2015. https://www.chalkbeat.org/posts/tn/2015/07/22/tennessee-teacher-training-programs-strive-to-bridge-culture-racial-gaps-in-the-classroom/.

Tomasek, Kathryn, Scott Hamlin, Zephorene Stickney, and Megan Wheaton-Book. "Discipline-Specific Learning and Collaboration in the Wheaton College Digital History Project." *Academic Commons*. August 25, 2015. http://www.academiccommons.org/2014/08/25/discipline-specific-learning-and-collaboration-in-the-wheaton-college-digital-history-project/.

Tufte, Edward. *The Visual Display of Quantitative Information*. 2nd ed. Cheshire, CT: Graphics Press, 2001.

Walvoord, Barbara, and Virginia Johnson Anderson. *Effective Grading: A Tool for Learning and Assessment in College*. 2nd ed. San Francisco: Jossey-Bass, 2009.

Whiteside, Aimee, D. Christopher Brooks, and J. Walker. "Making the Case for Space: Three Years of Empirical Research on Learning Environments." *EDUCAUSE Quarterly* 33 (September 2010).

Wieman, Carl. "Large-Scale Comparison of Science Teaching Methods Sends Clear Message." *Proceedings of the National Academy of Science* 111, no. 23 (June 2014), 8319–20.

Wiggins, Grant, and Jay McTighe. *Understanding by Design*. 2nd ed. Alexandria, VA: Association for Supervision and Curriculum Development, 2005.

Willmott, Chris. "Teaching Bioethics via the Production of Student-Generated Videos." *Journal of Biological Education* 49, no. 2 (2014): 127–38.

Wright, Leigh. "Tweet Me a Story." In *Web Writing: How and Why for Liberal Arts Teaching and Learning*, edited by Jack Dougherty and Tennyson O'Donnell. Ann Arbor: University of Michigan Press, 2014.

Young, Jeff. "Actually Going to Class, for a Specific Course? How 20th-Century." *Chronicle of Higher Education*. February 27, 2011. https://www.chronicle.com/article/Actually-Going-to-Class-How /126519.

Index